VARDAN

About the Author

Serge Momjian was born in Beirut in 1946. He moved to London in the 1970s and studied journalism then took a degree course in creative writing.

He has worked as a reporter, covering arts and culture for major publications, including Beirut's *Daily Star* (the Middle East's leading English-language newspaper) and London's *Events* magazine. His feature articles have been translated and published in the Armenian press. By the time he reached his forties, he was devoting his time to writing novels. His works, all published in the United Kingdom, include *Conflicting Motives*, *The Invisible Line*, *The Singer of the Opera*, *Memories of the Past*, *Komitas: The Artist and The Martyr*, *Gateway to Armenia* and *Tigranes the Great: The Rise and Fall of an Ancient Empire*.

In recognition of his biographical *Komitas* book, which included dialogue for the first time and was written in commemoration of the centenary of the Armenian Genocide, he was awarded the William Saroyan medal in 2015 by the Ministry of Diaspora of the Republic of Armenia (RA). The work will be translated into Armenian by Edit Print Publishing House in Yerevan. During his literary career his innovative writings have brought him praise and a good reputation.

VARDAN
Armenian Supreme Commander

451 AD, The Battle of Avarayr
- A faith victory

By Serge Momjian

HEDDON PUBLISHING
United Kingdom

First published in Great Britain 2022 by Heddon Publishing

www.heddonpublishing.com

Copyright © Serge Momjian 2022

A catalogue record for this book is available from the British Library

ISBN 978-1-913166-60-1

All rights reserved. No part of this publication may be reproduced, stored in a retrieval system or transmitted in any form or by any means, electric, mechanical, photocopying, recording or otherwise, without the prior permission of the publisher.

This is ancient military work based on true history with real historical characters. Includes appendices for data, maps and images.

The right of Serge Momjian to be identified as the author of this work has been asserted by him in accordance with the Copyright, Designs and Patents Act 1988.

Cover Design: Serge Momjian and Catherine Clarke

Cover images from knights of Vardan and Dreamstime.
Appendices images from Wikpedia/Wikimedia.

A Note to the Reader

The genre of the book is non-fiction/ancient military based on true history with real historical figures. As explained in the Introduction, I have included in the story corroborated dialogue and speech. Some of the former is partly representative but placed in the historical context. The idea is to bring the ancient world and the main characters to life.

It is hoped that this work will meet the historical interests of the readers who may never have read about the military life of the supreme Armenian commander – Vardan Mamikonian.

Contents

PART ONE
Chapter 1	The partition of Armenia
Chapter 2	The reign of King Tiridates III
Chapter 3	The tortures of St Gregory
Chapter 4	Gregory's incarceration and executions of the nuns
Chapter 5	Tiridates' transformation into a wild boar and the rescue of Gregory from the dungeon
Chapter 6	The conversion of Armenia to Christianity
Chapter 7	The journey of Tiridates and Gregory to Rome
Chapter 8	The Mamikonian great family

PART TWO
Chapter 9	The discovery of the Armenian alphabet
Chapter 10	The martyrdom of St Sarkis
Chapter 11	The accession of Yazdegerd I to the Sasanian throne
Chapter 12	The change of Yazdegerd's peaceful policy
Chapter 13	The abolition of the Arsacid dynasty of Armenia
Chapter 14	The translation of the Bible into Armenian
Chapter 15	The reign of the Shah Yazdegerd II
Chapter 16	His attempt to impose Zoroastrianism on Christians
Chapter 17	Audience with Armenian leaders and their imprisonment

Chapter 18	The release of the Armenian leaders from prison
Chapter 19	Preparation for the battle of Avarayr and Vardan's speech
Chapter 20	All-out confrontation between Armenian and Persian forces
Chapter 21	Estimation of casualties on both sides
Chapter 22	Yazdegerd's failure to assimilate the Armenians into the Mazdian religion and Yeghishe's experiences in the Battle of Avarayr
Epilogue	Page 137
Appendices	Page 147-177

Main Characters

Vardan Mamikonian: Armenian Supreme Commander

Tiridates III: King of Arsacid Armenia

Gregory the Illuminator: Patron saint

Mesrop Mashtots: Inventor of the Armenian alphabet

Yazdegerd I: King of the Sasanian Empire

Movses Khorenatsi: Armenian historian

Yazdegerd II: The Sasanian King of Kings

Cover Images

In the centre: Vardan

Bottom-left: The cross

Bottom-right: Fire temple built during the Sasanian reign

Introduction

Vardan Mamikonian was the supreme commander of the Armenian armed forces from 432 to 451 AD, following the partition of Ancient Armenia for over four decades earlier, between the Byzantine and Persian Empires. The nakharars (Armenian nobility) themselves had also been divided into two political camps, pro-Byzantine and pro-Persian, with both sides competing for absolute power. This resulted in the abolition of the Armenian kingship over the following decades, and the emergence of Marzbans (border guardians). Armenia was located at a strategic point, and found itself caught between the conflicting interests of its two powerful neighbours, Byzantium and Persia, with around eighty per cent of Armenian territory falling under the domination of the latter.

Both powers regarded Armenians as a threat to their expansionist policies in the region, and considered Armenian territory necessary to be conquered and its people subjugated. The division of Armenia not only interrupted the economic life of the whole country, but also led to the weakening of the position of the Armenian

Church, and its clergy was well aware of this fact.

Over the previous centuries, Zoroastrianism in the region had lingered on, with the succession of Persian kings, but in 301 AD, Armenia became the first nation to officially adopt Christianity as its state religion. That was almost a decade before Constantine the Great declared Christianity the religion of the Roman Empire. He issued the Edict of Milan, which allowed Christians to follow their faith without oppression, and to obtain confiscated Church property.

The Gospel had been preached in Armenia in the first century by two Apostles, St Thaddeus and St Bartholomew, and the two saints were ultimately martyred. The spread of the Christian religion by their followers was not an easy task. It was a long, protracted process, as the nation by and large still followed Zoroastrianism.

Various religions emerged at the end of the third century, each of which was linked to particular segments of society. At the same time, proselytizing Roman morals and beliefs would be viewed negatively. However, the old Zoroastrian religion was deeply rooted, especially in the Persian Armenians, and so did not disappear entirely, holding out for the next several decades.

In 298 AD, King Tiridates III – an ally of Rome and true to his pagan roots – had impiously persecuted and executed the Christians in Armenia, as disturbers of the social order. However, he eventually embraced Christianity, after a miraculous healing from his evil deeds by divine intervention, and then struggled to impose his new faith on the pagan people. The Gospel came to be honoured by the king, but not by all the Armenian nakharars. Some of them were in favour, others against it.

However, this marked the end of Paganism in Armenia, and

the beginning of the confiscation of all the old temple treasuries, followed by the laying of the foundation of the Holy Armenian Church. Ultimately, Tiridates' reign determined the course of much of Armenia's subsequent history.

Even Yazdegerd I, the Sasanian King of Kings – a Zoroastrian himself, but a peaceful ruler – promoted Christianity, in the early years of his reign, around 399 AD. He allowed the empire's Christians and Jews to practise their faith freely. The king issued a decree for the Assyrian Church, which permitted Christians to rebuild their churches, and bishops to travel freely in their dioceses. Moreover, he did good deeds, helping the poor and the wretched, who praised him, and prayed daily for his safety.

The nobility and priesthood in Persia did not approve of his new friendly relations with the religious minorities. But the king was determined to proceed with his tolerance of the Christian faith, and prevented the nobility from obtaining immoderate influence at the expense of royal power.

This period marked a new era for Armenia, making the fifth century the Golden Age of Armenian literature. Two major developments took place: the creation of the Armenian alphabet by Mesrop Mashtots, and later the translation of the Bible into Armenian. It was an era in which Vramshapuh, the previous Sasanian client king of Arsacid Armenia, was materially and morally the literacy project's great patron.

When King Yazdegerd II took his throne in about 438 AD, Roman influence on Armenia and the issue of Christianity came to a head, with the reappointment of Mihr Narseh as chief-minister. The king – a ruthless Zoroastrian fanatic – had again forced all the empire's Christians, namely

Armenians, to renounce Christianity, and convert back to Zoroastrianism. The issue of the Christian religion opened the gap of ambivalence between the pro-Roman Armenian religious camp under Byzantine influence, and the pro-Zoroastrian camp, which had heavy Sasanid influence. Yazdegerd's aim was to better assimilate Armenia into his realm, by reducing Greek influence, and even forbidding Greek culture. This greatly appeased the Persian aristocracy, as well as the Zoroastrian priesthood.

After a decree was sent out, the Armenian bishops, led by St Leontius and Vardan, called a council at Artashad, where they unanimously and stubbornly defended their culture, and Christian religion. They sent their declaration of faith to the king, who became increasingly enraged and issued further threats. As a result of the arbitrary commands, Vardan (a devoted Christian) led a sizeable Armenian rebellion against their Sasanian overlords in the eastern provinces.

The Armenian rebel leader strongly repudiated the Zoroastrian religion, and his partisans attacked the temples and shrines, killing many priests. A faction of the Armenian nobility led by Vasak Siuni – a Marzban prince – defected, and allied themselves with the Sasanians against the rebellions. The prince presented himself as a mediator, but was hated by his compatriots for his Mazdian sympathies.

The virulent attack on the Magians, who were so ill-received by Vardan's people, and in some cases massacred, continued until the capture of important cities – Garni and Artagert – by the rebels, and the execution of the chief of the Magians and his son. This prompted a furious reaction from Yazdegerd, who marched his massive army, with war elephants, to Armenia under his top general, Mushkan

Nusalavurd. With Vardan as the supreme commander of the armed forces, the countdown to the crucial, heroic battle of Avarayr in 451 AD had begun.

Vardan Mamikonian is much mentioned in the writings of various historians, academicians, scholars and researchers, especially in modern Armenian literary works and the media. I have been inspired to write about this national hero firstly because of his great dedication to being a faithful Christian commander. Against the backdrop of antagonism by the Sasanians, Vardan led his army in one of the first holy battles in the history of Christendom, highlighting the idealism of the Armenian people in defending their principles. Secondly, no book has been written about him that incorporates dialogue, both in his story and in the periods before and after the division of Armenia in 387 AD.

The present work is based on true history, with real historical characters, and gives fresh insights into the Battle of Avarayr. I have added corroborated dialogue and speech to the story – some of the former is representative, to bring Vardan and past events to life. Parts of the book, related to Byzantine and Christendom in the fourth century, are based on reliable sources – Armenian, Greek, and Latin chronicles and documents. I avoided, as much as possible, using too many names and dates, in order to enable readers to remember and connect with the story.

Writing history means going into considerable detail, but in regard to each period I have endeavoured to give a relatively condensed description of the evolution of Armenia's socio-political structure from the third to the fifth centuries, and its relations with the major two powers – the Eastern Roman and Persian Empires. There are a couple of different written interpretations of the events that occurred, especially during the reign of Tiridates III. I disagree with these made-up stories, which to my mind do not correspond to reality whatsoever.

To give the reader a description of what marked a turning point in the history of Armenia, the second chapter in the novel starts with a flashback to a series of significant events that led up to the rise of the Mamikonian family, and eventually to the military life of their supreme commander – Vardan. To put it simply, the story in Part One, Chapter 1 continues in Part Two, Chapter 9.

S.M

PART ONE

Chapter 1

In 387 AD, an agreement had been signed between the Sasanian King Shapur III and the Roman Emperor Theodosius I, to partition Armenia into two sectors: Western Armenia to be under Byzantium rule, and Eastern or Persian Armenia to remain a kingdom under Sasanid rule. Known as the Peace of Acilisene, the boundary line stretched through Theodosiopolis in the north and Amida (Dyarbakir) in the south. Thus, the much greater share of the disputed territory was left to the Persian Sasanids, including the northern and north-western provinces adjacent to Iberia and Colchis.

In fact, the concept of the division of Armenia had come about a year earlier, when the kingdom was in turmoil over continuing disputes, between some of the nobility who gave their backing to the king appointed by the Romans, and others who preferred a ruler appointed by the Persians. Two nakharar clans became engaged in confrontation – the Artsrunis, and the Mamikonians. The internal struggle and the wavering loyalties of the Armenian nobility, the king, and the clergy eventually accelerated this division of Armenia.

Shapur III was the son of Shapur II. Back in 379 AD, he had designated his half-brother Ardashir II as his successor, on condition that he would resign when his son reached adulthood. But Ardashir's reign ended after only four years, when he was killed by the Iranian nobility. The reason behind this was his continuation of Shapur II's policy of restricting the authority of power-hungry nobles. Shapur III, who succeeded him, was well received by his subjects, pleased that the crown had been given to offspring of Shapur II. The latter had once declared to them in his accession speech that he would not allow deceit, greed, or self-righteousness at his court. However, this was unacceptable to the nobility. Apart from the dispute over Armenia, the new Sasanian King of Kings had clashed with the Alchon Huns to the east.

Arshak III, a prince who served as Roman client of Arsacid Armenia, was forced to withdraw to the western sector of Armenia, after Shapur had sent an invasion force into its eastern sector. In the city of Ekeghiats, the prince was given Roman protection, but in turn his dominion was much reduced. He died in his young age a few years later, without leaving an heir, and his realm was annexed to the Byzantine Empire. As a result, the western part of Armenia became a province, and lost its independence and status of kingdom.

The Byzantines had administratively divided their portion of Armenia into northern and southern sections: Armenia I in the north and Armenia II in the south. In both sectors, each with a governor, members of the Armenian nobility were included in the administration. The internal status of the western part of Armenia had remained unchanged, with its native social order and laws. Ultimately, the political agreement by the two major powers not only divided

Armenia into geographic areas, but also separated its Christian communities. As a result, a faction of the Armenians who lived in Western Armenia, including most of the nobility, moved into Eastern Armenia.

Those nobles, who already lived in the eastern sector under Sasanian rule, appealed to King Shapur for another successor. He willingly responded by crowning Khosrov IV, a prince from the Arsacid Dynasty, as King of Arsacid Armenia. To extend his courtesies, Shapur gave his sister Zruanduxt, a Sasanian princess, to Khosrov in marriage. As a queen consort, she became a powerful and influential woman, with an army provided by her brother to protect Armenia. Shapur also allowed the Christian minorities to worship freely in his empire. As a result, his religious policy contributed to stabilizing relations with the Romans, as well as conciliating the Armenians themselves.

It was during this period that an Armenian noble family known as Kamsarakans, under their leader Gazavon II Kamsarak, also moved with their family members to the Sasanian sector. One of the seven great Houses of Persia claiming Arsacid origin, the family had reigned in two princely states, both situated in the region of Ararat. Due to the geographical location of their principalities, they were not specifically involved in Armenian-Persian relations. Rather, they were known for following a broadly pro-Byzantine policy, and involved in the political life of the empire.

With the peace treaty of Acilisene, the Romans fully acknowledged Persian hegemony over Eastern Armenia. Both sides were to cooperate in the defence of the Caucasus, with the Romans agreeing to provide the Persians with political allocations at irregular intervals. Thereafter, Arsacid rule brought about an intensification of Persia's political and cultural influence on Armenia. Together with Iberia and Albania, the country was now part of a pan-Arsacid family federation.

The Armenian branch of the Arsacid dynasty, whose kings maintained close ties to Persia, had intermittently continued ruling the Kingdom of Armenia from 12 AD, and later as a Sasanian vassal. The Artsrunis reigned in the princely states of Greater and Lesser Albak, southeast of Lake Van. The political weight of this feudal house was the aid which it had to render to its king, consisting of over 1000 soldiers. For almost four centuries, the Arsacids managed to keep their balance on the diplomatic tightrope strung between the great powers of Persia and Eastern Roman Byzantine.

Eastern Armenia was governed by a client monarch, under Sasanian hegemony, whose official religion was Zoroastrianism. The Sasanians, who selected each ruling viceroy, had mostly left the two key institutions of the Armenian state untouched: the nakharars (nobility) and the church. The former were local princes, whose ranks and titles were based on the hereditary clans of Ancient Armenia, who governed their own extensive lands as semi-autonomous fiefdoms. Some, however, had switched loyalties to the Persians, even converting to Zoroastrianism, in exchange for tax and other privileges.

King Khosrov bestowed Sahak (Isaac) Partev of Parthian origin as Armenian Patriarch and appointed Mesrop Mashtots as his imperial secretary. Using Greek and Persian characters, Mesrop wrote the decrees and edicts of the kingdom. Moreover, he restored nakharars to their former nobility status. Mesrop was well known for his sympathies towards the Byzantine Empire, and to

Theodosius I and his family.

After his election, Isaac worked closely and actively with King Khosrov, to restore the unity of Greater Armenia. Having received a high literary education in Constantinople, particularly in Eastern languages, the patriarch had a wide knowledge of phonetics, and rhetorical commentary, and was well-versed in philosophy. He devoted himself to the religious and scientific training of his people. In the Byzantine territory, the Greek language was used, whereas in the Persian sector Greek was prohibited, and Syriac greatly favoured.

Shapur III died in 388 AD, having reigned for a little more than five years. In one of his palace courts, he had erected a large tent, which fell on him when some nobles cut its ropes. He was succeeded by his son, Bahram IV, who quickly dispatched an embassy to Theodosius, to confirm the validity of the agreement reached in the preceding year, which might have lapsed after the death of his father.

Bahram dethroned Khosrov a year later, and placed him in confinement in Ctsesiphon, for being too self-confident in his royal authority as a governing client monarch, and having committed acts in his kingship without approval from the Sasanid court. The main reason for Khosrov's removal was his appointment of Sahak as the patriarch of Eastern Armenia, without the consent of the court. Bahram replaced Khosrov with his brother, Vramshapuh, to serve as a Sasanian client king of Arsacid Armenia. But there was a problem at the time, due to Armenia's feudalism, which was relentlessly weakening the integrity of the state. Moreover, the political/military events and geographic diversity greatly reinforced the nobility's decentralized system. The country was passing through a great crisis, its ancient culture in danger of disappearing, and national unity was seriously compromised.

The attempts to strengthen Vramshapuh's absolute power met resistance from the nobility and the Church. The king, realizing the great difficulty of establishing relations with the former, tried to reduce these tensions by adopting a policy of appeasement and reconciliation. He was particularly aiming to maintain peaceful relations with Persia and Byzantium, and later to mediate between the two empires. Vramshapuh was finally able to establish a long-lasting peace, which contributed to the internal improvement of the region, into which Christianity had penetrated, and kept the spread of pagan faiths to a minimum.

Chapter 2

Back in 298 AD, the Roman-Armenian alliance had grown stronger, especially when the Emperor Diocletian ruled the Eastern Roman Empire. His reign stabilized the empire, and marked the end of the Crisis of the Third Century. He had much earlier appointed fellow officer Maximian as Augustus, co-emperor, who reigned in the Western Empire. Diocletian had delegated further, appointing Galerius and Constantius as junior co-emperors, under himself and Maximian respectively. Under the "rule of four", each emperor would rule over a quarter-division of the empire. Diocletian first secured the borders and purged the empire of all threats to his power. He defeated the Sarmatians, the Alamanni, and usurpers in Egypt during several campaigns. He then separated and enlarged the empire's civil and military services, and reorganized the provincial divisions, establishing the largest and most bureaucratic government, with new administrative centres closer to the empire's frontiers than the traditional capital at Rome.

As a self-styled autocrat, he elevated himself above the empire's masses, with imposing forms of court ceremonies.

Bureaucratic and military growth, constant campaigning, and construction projects increased the state's expenditure, necessitating a comprehensive tax reform.

With Diocletian's help in the face of persistent Persian aggressions, Tiridates III ascended to the throne of Greater Armenia, which had been deprived of its independence for a quarter of a century. The new Arsacid monarch, a loyal ally of the Roman Emperor, was married to an Alani Princess called Ashkhen – a member of the Arsacid dynasty – who became the Queen of Armenia, by whom he had three children: a son called Khosrov III, and two daughters, one of them called Salome. An impious king, Tiridates drove the Persians out of his domains, but did not break off all links with them. Diocletian left the Armenian state with quasi-independent and protectorate status, to use it as a buffer zone in case of any Persian attack.

During this period, monotheism was considered an offensive worship against polytheism. The emperor had issued several edicts, one of them stipulating that all subjects of his empire must comply with traditional Roman religious practices, such as sacrifice to the Roman gods. Some people refused to participate in the Roman Imperial cult. Considering it an act of treason, they were subjected to persecution, imprisonment, torture, and death. Moreover, their homes were demolished, and their sacred books collected and burned.

Gregory, the son of a Parthian noble named Anak, and one of the infants saved from a slaughter in Armenia, was rushed by his nurse to the city of Caesarea in Cappadocia, where he was brought up as a Christian. He accepted Christianity and returned to Armenia, as part of a mission sanctioned by the Church in Cappadocia.

At that time, Armenia by and large followed Paganism rather than Zoroastrianism, but some Christians practised their faith in secret. The whole nation followed various religions, which were a mix of local Iranian and Hellenistic cults. There were Iranian and Pagan centres of cults throughout the territory, which honoured important deities, such as Anahit, Aramazd (Ahuramazda), and Mihr (Mithras).

Gregory knew that his own father, Anak, had greatly wronged the Armenian people by murdering King Tiridates' father. Feeling guilt for this, he joined the Armenian army. King Tiridates learned that Gregory was a well-educated, dependable, conscientious young man, and he wanted him to become his secretary. To make amends for what his father had done, Gregory accepted the post without ever revealing his parentage.

During a great votive religious celebration in Eriza, the king, a pagan worshipper himself, commanded his secretary with a half-smile: 'Gregory, give an offering to Anahit, the most popular deity in the country.'

Gregory shook his head. 'No.'

'Just lay a wreath at the foot of her statue,' the king suggested.

'I refuse to pay homage to an idol goddess,' Gregory replied politely.

The king now had a grim look, and the atmosphere changed. Murmurs of disapproval passed through the crowd. 'Who does he think he is, defying the king?' 'How can he dare to talk the way he does?' Some whispered to each other, 'He's the king's secretary.'

As a result of Gregory's act of disobedience, the king, his brows drawn together, said, 'You've served me well all these years, why do you refuse now to do my will?'

'Yes, I've served you, because God commands us to serve our earthly lords at all times,' Gregory replied calmly. He continued, 'If we believe in one God, the only creator of heaven and earth, we must then worship Him as our sovereign Lord.'

'What an absurd thing to say!' the king exclaimed.

'Absolutely not. He is the true life and light for those who are in the darkness of idolatry. So, I urge you to abandon false worship, and follow the teachings of Christ.'

The king became so uneasy about Gregory's comments that he wanted to forget his relationship with him for a while, and concentrate instead on consolidating his reign in the empire, which was in a distracted state.

Tiridates had a sharp recollection of the events that had led up to the tragic murder of his father, King Khosrov II. The latter, with his army and a large crowd of Caucasian tribes who had come to his aid, had ravaged the lands under Persian rule, destroying the fortified cities and settlements. The Parthians, having attached themselves to the Persian King Artashir, refused to help Khosrov. In the following months, Khosrov, emerging victorious, returned to the city of Vagharshapat, the capital of the Arsacid Kingdom of Armenia, where he celebrated his conquests and rewarded all his soldiers. He honoured his ancestral worship sites and the temples of the idol-worshipping cults.

He then reassembled his armies, and plundered far-reaching Persian lands. Artashir could not withstand the pressure of his enemy's troops.

The Persian king summoned to his royal court all the princes, nobles and governors of his kingdom, so that he could find a man to take vengeance against this vicious

Khosrov. He promised he would elevate such a man to the second rank in the kingdom, and bestow many gifts and rewards upon him, if he should succeed in avenging him.

Among the king's council there was a Parthian noble named Anak, of the Suren family, who offered to carry out the vengeance. The Parthian went to Vagharshapat, where he formulated a plan to meet Khosrov alone.

The king received him gladly, and passed the last winter days with him in happiness. After winning Khosrov's trust, thoughts of the Persian king's promise stirred in Anak's mind. In 258 AD, he raised his sword, and struck Khosrov dead. Outraged, the Armenian princes split into groups, scoured the countryside, captured the killer, and threw his body from a bridge, into the waters of the Arax River. After that, they slaughtered the family of the Parthian noble.

Tiridates, a child and the only heir to the throne, knew about the appalling attack on his father. To avoid falling into the hands of the Persians, he fled Armenia, and was sent to Rome, where he was educated and provided with military training. After fighting in the Roman army for years, he personally led his own army to victories in many battles. He was such a brave and promising warrior that he received his crown from Nero, to become King of Armenia. After the coronation, friendly relations were established between Rome and the kingdom of Armenia.

In time, the king was stunned when one of the courtiers disclosed to him Gregory's true identity, as the son of the notorious Anak, who had killed Tiridates' father. The king also learned that his secretary was preaching Christianity – something he had not known before; nor did he know that the preacher was another infant survivor from the raid.

Chapter 3

Tiridates had Gregory brought up to his court, to provide an explanation for his religious conduct. Leaving aside the issue of Anak for a while, the king scowled at Gregory and said, 'How many times have I told you not to repeat these absurd tales of yours, which are not fit to be heard? You've insulted the great Anahid, who always protects life in our land, and the brave Aramazd, our creator of heaven and earth, and the giver of prosperity. As for the other gods, you've called them simple things, without breath or speech, and you said they should be destroyed.'

Gregory remained silent, while the king stared at him in anger and went on, 'You've also insulted us by calling us horses and mules that have no understanding whatsoever; no thought to search for God. Therefore, in return for all these insults, I will give you over to my men, to subject you to harsh tortures.'

The king ordered his men to take Gregory to his palace's dungeon, where they should put a bit in his mouth and lie him down with his face to the floor. After tying his hands behind his back, they should place a heavy chunk of salt upon his shoulders. Having carried out their king's orders, the men harnessed Gregory like a donkey, and kept him that way for two days.

The man endured the king's disgraceful conduct in pain, hunger and privation.

On the third day, the king commanded Gregory to be hung by one foot, and all manner of filth to be burnt under his head. Thus, he remained suspended, with his head down, for seven days, during which time five men in succession beat him. Gregory asked God for strength and grace to endure the torments. The stench that continually rose from under him almost choked him, but he did not utter a groan, for raising once more his mind to God in the deepest thoughts, he was filled with inexpressible consolation.

In the following week, the king ordered his men to bring two wooden clubs, both the size of a shinbone, to be fitted together like the bars of a wine press. Having placed Gregory's legs in between them, the men tied the bones tight with ropes, then twisted them until blood gushed out and over their fingers. Gregory, determined not to deny and forsake Christ, looked heavenward, and gave himself over to the tormentors.

After a couple of days, the king came to his prisoner and cast a disdainful look at him. 'How are you, Gregory? How did you bear all that? Have you yet any consciousness, or felt any pain?'

Gregory replied soberly, 'I asked the Lord to give me the strength to bear this torture, and He gave it to me.'

'Be convinced that I'm right, and come to the great gods. If you do not, I swear that with their glorious power I will destroy you.'

Gregory replied firmly, 'I will come, but to my God only.'

'Have you not yet understood it is in vain that you believe in your god? Otherwise, show me what good it has done for you.'

'I believe in my God, who is merciful, and my refuge. I'm ready to accept death, whatever you do to my body.'

The following day, the king, frustrated by his failure to make Gregory bow to his will and respect the worship of the idols, inflicted yet more cruel tortures. He ordered his men this time to boil together nitre, salt, and strong vinegar, after which he instructed them to place the prisoner on his back, and put his head in a vice. Turning the screw with a bar, the hot mixture should be then poured into the prisoner's nostrils through reeds, as he drew his breath.

The king's men did as they were instructed, and while the prisoner moaned, Tiridates hoped that it might disturb Gregory's brain, and force him to worship the idols.

As this method of torture also failed, and the king was determined to impose his will upon Gregory, he stubbornly continued, devising new ways to torture the prisoner. In order to choke his breathing completely, boiling water was poured onto Gregory's stomach. He let out a groan, but did not die.

Later that day, on the king's orders, a basketful of iron spikes was brought in and spread thick over the ground. The king's men placed Gregory naked on those spikes, dragged him over them, and rolled him about until his whole body was pierced through, and the ground was covered with blood. The prisoner gave a terrible groan, but knew that if he endured undeserved suffering, God would bless him for it.

The king drew near and asked mockingly, 'Where's your god, Gregory, in whom you trusted? Shall he now come and deliver you from my hand?'

Gregory, who with remarkable patience and by the power of the Lord had remained alive, murmured in the king's ear, 'You see, the more my outward body perished, the more I was renewed inwardly, and came again into earthly existence.'

'Oh, really?' the king said, in mock-surprise.

After a pause, Gregory went on, 'If anyone in this world does not repent and turn back to Christ, the person should prepare himself to face His final judgment: eternity in Heaven for those who put their faith in Him, or in Hell for the wicked.'

'You're telling me more absurd tales now,' the king rebuked.

Gregory shook his head. 'No.' He then remained silent.

Tiridates turned his fury on him. 'Because of your continued intransigence in fulfilling my wishes, and to avenge the murder of my father by your father, I will throw you into a deep dungeon, where you shall know your deluded world, and starve to death.'

The next morning, Tiridates' men took the prisoner to Khor Virap (an Armenian monastery located in the Ararat plain). On the king's orders, Gregory's hands and legs were tied, and he was imprisoned in a deep underground cell, which is still in existence today. The cell – infamous for torture at that time – writhed with snakes, scorpions and insects, and reeked of decaying flesh. It was not the kind of prison from which people returned.

While Tiridates was flourishing, Gregory remained in the pit that had killed all other prisoners condemned to it, because of the dangerous snakes, filth and stench. The haughty king, who was exceedingly brave, daring, and very proud, continued devastating the Persian kingdom.

Chapter 4

At sunset, following Gregory's incarceration, a devoted woman sent by the Lord lowered into the pit by rope a small bucket containing a single loaf of bread soaked in water, along with some cheese. 'I will come back tomorrow and every day, to keep you alive,' she said, her voice echoing through the hole. With hands and legs untied through divine intervention, and poisonous snakes/scorpions turned into harmless creatures, the prisoner ate a piece of the bread and joined God in his prayer. 'O Lord, here I am, thrown into a pit at no fault of my own. Thank you for everything you have bestowed upon me, for providing food for me today. Your blessed name be glorified forever.'

Tiridates – an implacable foe of the Christian faith – had issued two edicts showing how dangerous Christianity was for the pagan religion in the country. The first decreed that Christians pay proper homage to the gods, the second that those who dared to hide Christians be put to death, reminding his subjects of the severe way he had dealt with Gregory.

During this period, Emperor Diocletian, who was seeking a wife, sent painters out to find lovely women and bring back portraits of them, so that he could choose from these pictures a beautiful wife for himself.

One of the painters found a group of nuns living a monastic life. Their abbess was named Gayane.

Immediately attracted by the beauty of a particular young nun, the painter completed her portrait and rushed to the emperor to show it to him.

'Take a look at this beautiful girl,' the painter said as he handed her portrait to the emperor.

'A nun!' Captivated by her beauty, Diocletian asked, 'What's her name?'

'Hripsime. She is of Roman origin.'

'Oh, really? That is eminently suitable for me.' After giving it some thought, the emperor went on, 'Well, I think she will no longer be a nun, from now on.'

The emperor offered the painter gifts for his service and, infatuated by Hripsime's beauty, decided to arrange a grand wedding.

Meanwhile, Diocletian's vanity led him to persecute the Christian Church leaders, in order to show his power over them. He issued an edict calling for the burning of all their sacred writings, the imprisonment of priests, bishops and deacons, and obligatory sacrifice to the Roman gods.

Hripsime, who heard about the wave of persecution, and learned that she was to be forcefully married, was joined by the abbess and other nuns in fleeing the tyrant emperor. They came to Vagharshabat – the residence of the Armenian kings. In the same city, King Tiridates, who had been in contact with Rome, received an emissary from his friend, Diocletian, who said in his letter:

'I think my brother, Tiridates, knows the evils that constantly beset us. I am referring to this error-ridden

Christian sect who worship a dead man, adore a cross on which he was crucified, and consider their own death to be glory and honour. They have rejected the power of the sun, moon and stars, and everywhere among our people they discourage the worship of our gods. Threats and punishments against them are completely futile.

'I happened to see among a group of nuns a lovely, beautiful girl, named Hripsime. I wanted to have her as my wife, but she and her companions insulted me by fleeing to the regions of your kingdom. So, my brother, find them for me, and send this virgin back to me, unless you wish to keep her for yourself.'

Tiridates immediately ordered a search, and discovered the nuns' hiding place. As word of the emperor's edict had spread across the land, there were soon crowds of people straining to catch a glimpse of the beautiful nun. She and her companions offered constant prayers, and wished only to live a holy and solitary life.

The king sent magnificent robes to Hripsime, so that she could adorn herself before coming to his palace. The group of nuns were escorted to him by soldiers and, along the way, the abbess tried to strengthen Hripsime in her resistance to the king. 'Remember, my child, you have longed for the never-ending life of the Kingdom of Christ. Don't give up your choice now, and don't yield your holy virtue to these infidels.'

The king was enthralled by the unique beauty of Hripsime, and, wanting to have her as his concubine, he pointed to her. 'Stay here,' he said calmly, and gestured for the other nuns to leave.

When they left, Hripsime acknowledged the king's advances and shook her head firmly. 'No.'

'If you reject my kindness, you and your companions will be subjected to great sufferings and death,' he warned.

Hripsime, determined not to renounce her Christian faith, managed to escape from the palace, and joined the nuns' dwelling place. In the meantime, Nino, another member of the community of nuns, escaped persecution in Armenia and fled to Caucasian Iberia (now Georgia), where she experienced an apparition of the Virgin Mary, who encouraged her to preach Christianity.

Tiridates ordered his soldiers to capture the group of nuns and have them mercilessly tortured and killed. Hripsime's tongue was to be cut out first, then Gayane and two other nuns beheaded, and the rest of the community put to the sword. Having carried out the king's strict orders, the soldiers dragged the women's bodies out and cast them away on the mountains, as food for the prowling dogs.

Chapter 5

Tiridates was in emotional distress, and suffered pangs of conscience for having slaughtered innocent beings. To distract himself from thinking about his gruesome act, the king went hunting, but he fell suddenly from the horse, as if struck down by divine providence as a punishment for his evil deeds. He became totally insane, and adopted the behaviour of a wild boar, with a fierce face, grinding his teeth and grunting, aimlessly roaming around the forest. His sister, Khosrovidukht, was quickly informed of what was happening, and rushed to the forest, where she looked for her brother everywhere. She was startled by a sudden grunt, and stepped backwards. She saw her brother at a slight distance, and moved cautiously towards him, but he growled, threatening her with his teeth bared. She froze in place, stupefied.

'What in the name of gods and goddesses is happening to you, brother?' she asked, disgusted.

Seeing him in that awful state, she realized there was no way to bring him back to his senses. She returned home, spending the night in torment, wondering which demon had possessed her brother. In time, she had a vision, wherein an angel told her that Gregory was still alive in the pit, and that he could heal her brother. This dream came to her repeatedly, and she told a prince about the good news.

'He's still alive? And you think he could heal your brother?' he asked in astonishment. 'After thirteen years of imprisonment, no one could ever come out of that pit alive.'

Nevertheless, Khosrovidukht, placing much faith in the angel's words, sent the prince to Khor Virap with clear instructions; to find someone who could pull the Christian man out of the dungeon, and take him to her brother.

Upon arrival, the prince said to himself, 'This is all ridiculous, the man must surely have died long ago.'

A crowd of curious villagers gathered at nearby St Kevork chapel – a small basilica with a semi-circular apse – to observe the event. The prince found a robust man, who volunteered to pull the Christian out of the pit. He went down with a length of rope into the chapel's last room, where a long stairway led down through a narrow, damp pit, to the bottom of a tiny, cylindrical cell, about fourteen feet wide. The man dropped the rope and called, 'Gregory, are you down there?' His voice reverberated in the pit. The man was amazed to feel a tug on the rope. He knew then that the prisoner was still alive, and he asked Gregory to tie the rope tightly around himself, so that he could be pulled out. The people outside stood astounded when they heard the man's shout, 'He's alive!'

A few moments later, Gregory emerged in a miserable state – with a long beard, worn-out clothes, and darkened face. The villagers helped him to get clean, and brought fresh clothing for him. They then took him to Tiridates, who had by now gone entirely mad, tearing his own skin.

Through exorcism and prayers of forgiveness from Gregory, the ailing king was miraculously healed from his illness, and restored to human form. He stared at his prisoner and quickly recognized him. Having realized that he was a victim of his own evil deeds, with tears welling in his eyes, he said regretfully, 'I'm truly sorry for the great suffering I have caused you, and for the Christian martyrs who gave their lives to keep their faith – all because of my shameful tyranny.'

Gregory converted the king and the royal family to Christianity, then left for Caesarea, where he was ordained a bishop by Leontius, the archbishop there. When Gregory returned to Armenia, he baptized Tiridates in his court with a purple mantle, but without a throne. The king knelt down before his holy rescuer, with his head down, hands clasping each other strongly in faith, while Gregory stood in full stature, a mitre on his head, dressed in a splendid religious robe.

The king raised his head and as he became a new man, he said, 'Your God is my God now, your religion is my religion.'

Gregory pulled him to his feet and said, 'I'm just a man like you, and the one who has had mercy on you is your creator, the Lord of all things.'

Shortly afterwards, Gregory baptized the king's whole royal household, and later his army, in the Euphrates River.

The next day, Gregory gathered up the remains of the holy martyred nuns – no dog had touched their bodies. He enshrouded them, and took them to the nuns' former dwelling place, where he had chapels built to house their relics.

The power of the miraculous cure by divine intervention, and the baptism of the king, forced Tiridates to make a very important announcement, in the presence of the local people gathered outside his palace. He stood on the steps and raised his arms, to show that he had something to say. When he had complete quiet, he began to speak. 'For long decades, we've been worshipping many statues of ancient gods and goddesses, and also fire, as a symbol of the pagan religion. I myself made sacrifices officially to the triad Aramazd-Anahit-Vahagn. But recently, I came to realize with much regret that all these deities we used to worship in temples were useless, for they couldn't do anything on their own.' After a short pause, he went on with absolute determination, 'From now on, we must believe in one God, so I proclaim Christianity the state religion of Armenia.'

Most of the people, astounded, deplored the king's announcement. Some of them started booing loudly. 'How can we worship one god?'

Others denounced the new religion, shouting its name with disdain. 'Christianity!'

The king dismissed all their complaints and returned to his palace.

Chapter 6

In 301 AD, Armenia became the first state in the world to officially embrace the Christian religion. During the days following Tiridates' announcement, Gregory had a vision of Jesus appearing as a heroic figure of light, descending from Heaven. Surrounded by a mighty angelic host, the son of God struck the ground with a golden hammer and the voice said, 'This is the place where the Mother Cathedral of the first Christian nation is to be established, and you will name it "The Descent of the Only-Begotten" [Etchmiatzin].'

The last words reverberated twice in Gregory's mind, and he replied firmly, 'I will fulfil your order. Let God's will be done.'

When the building of the church began, on the remains of a pagan temple, Tiridates appointed Gregory the Supreme Bishop of the Armenian Apostolic Church. Called the "Illuminator" and hailed as a saint, Gregory organized the hierarchy of the Church according to the principles of the Armenian state administrative system, and ordained a bishop for every principality. These bishops were under his jurisdiction. Eventually, St Gregory became the first Catholicos (the head of the Church) of all Armenians.

Christianization of Armenia by the religious leaders was not an easy task, as paganism was deeply rooted in its people. However, Tiridates and his supporters used the transition from polytheism to monotheism as a means to achieve greater political and economic power, and centralization. This monotheistic religion instilled greater loyalties from the nobility. The king strengthened the ministries and the Armenian Church, using the potential of the most notable nakharars, to whom he gave various extra positions and holdings. Given that the wars in nearby Armenia's borders were caused by dynastic incongruity, he avoided any military conflict with the Persians.

In 308 AD, the king prevented an invasion by the Roman Emperor Maximinus Daia, whose intention was to crush the newly established Christian religion in Armenia. The emperor retreated, and the country remained a Christian nation.

In the meantime, Gregory had told the native Armenian pagans the long history of God's salvation for mankind. He felt the need to continue the task of instructing his people – attentive and filled with wonder – and ever more of them started to live in a new way. Some pagans asked the Illuminator to intercede with his God to save them, for they feared that whenever he left, the demons would assail them again. But Gregory assured them that if they recognized his God, they would have no more fears. He told them how the Lord had changed the poisonous snakes in the pit into harmless creatures, so that he would be saved, and the people would see the power of the miracles. He succeeded in baptizing around four thousand men and women, thus converting them to Christianity.

Tiridates worked closely with Gregory to spread the Christian religion through their kingdom and to suppress the pagan cults, which, however, did not completely disappear. Both men travelled, escorted by a contingent of the king's army, throughout the various provinces, and converted more Armenians by accomplishing miracles.

It struck the king that he had to destroy another large, well-appointed temple at the city of Artashat, where he used to worship the patron gods and goddess – Aramazd, Vahagn, and Anahit. The journey there was halted for a short time, as an angel appeared and said, 'It has pleased God that the saints should soon dwell in Artashat.'

When they arrived in the city, they saw people still offering sacrifices to the same three deities in the temple. Gregory, realizing that it was not easy to batter down the mighty gates, held up his cross, saying, 'Let your angels drive the demons away, Lord.'

Howling, violent winds blew from the cross, and levelled the temple with the altars, leaving no trace of them. He turned to the pagan people. 'See, your stumbling blocks have been removed,' he said, while most of the onlookers stared open-mouthed at the scene and thus began to believe in the Lord.

Gregory and the king reused the site to build the first church, for the relics of John the Baptist, which were brought from Cappadocia. They then arranged a baptismal font, where Gregory remained with the people for a month and baptized them, converting each one to Christianity. This marked the beginning of his great efforts to provide every region with churches, and priests to perform services in them. The young evangelist willingly continued to spread the gospel message everywhere, helped those in distress and despair, and established monastic orders in the populace plains and isolated mountain caves. Armenian society began to understand that there was only one God in three divine persons – the Holy Trinity – Father, Son (Christ), and the Holy Spirit.

In 313 AD, the Roman Emperor Constantine the Great, who governed the whole empire, issued the Edict of Tolerance, also known as the Edict of Milan, which he co-authored with Licinius, and which allowed Christians to follow their faith without oppression. The edict removed all penalties for professing belief in Christianity – by which many had formerly been martyred – and returned confiscated Church property. The Christian martyrs had died for monotheistic beliefs, "One God against the many gods". It was a long struggle with the Roman Empire, which culminated in the victory of Christianity, and monotheism over polytheism. Christians now had the emperor's assurance, that they could rebuild with confidence their earlier churches, which had been destroyed or damaged. Constantine himself erected churches, with his imperial resources, like the Holy Sepulchre in Jerusalem, and the Holy Nativity in Bethlehem. With the emperor's continual support, construction of the Church of St John Lateran in Rome began, and the emperor forbade any cult statues and sacrifice. This new concept of the religious policy in Rome greatly improved relations between Armenia and the Roman Empire.

Constantine's conversion to Christianity not only brought stability and order to the empire, but provided him with a justification for the expansion of Roman absolute power, to be a Christian empire ruled by the emperor. Rome, seeking to control Armenia, saw the merit of permitting the spread of the Christian faith as a means to maintain the kingdom's independence from Persia.

Chapter 7

Tiridates was a tireless servant of the Lord in his witness to others, and in his spiritual life. He always observed feast days (days of celebration in the religious calendar) and fasts, and strove to do God's will.

The king learned that Gregory had two sons from a youthful marriage: Vertanes and Aristaces. The former was living a secular life, the latter an ascetical life of prayer, like a monk. Delighted by his discovery, Tiridates had them both brought to his court, after which he went with them to seek their father. Gregory was in the province of Daranalik, and had been absent from court for some time. He agreed to Tiridates' proposal to make Aristaces a bishop, so that his son could carry on his work.

A few weeks later, the king set out with Gregory and his sons, and some of the high-ranking members of the royal court. Travelling from Vagharshapat through Greek territory, they were honourably received along the way. Soon afterwards, they arrived in Rome, where Emperor Constantine and Patriarch Eusebius greeted them warmly. Following a lavish ceremony, when the emperor beseeched them to tell him about the miracles performed in Armenia, Tiridates explained all that had happened there, without withholding any details of his own bestial transformation.

Feeling so guilty over the sacrifice of the brave martyrs, the king introduced Gregory to the emperor, as the man through whom God's will had been done. Astonished by the story, and having Gregory's blessing, Constantine told Tiridates how he himself had come to know God. Moreover, he spoke about his war against the rival Roman pagan kings – Diocletian, Licinius, and Maxentius – and the rebuilding of the Christian churches they had destroyed during persecutions.

The name Diocletian rang twice in Tiridates' mind. For a brief moment, he unwillingly recalled with disdain what this man – once his friend, now his enemy – had said to him: 'This error-ridden Christian sect who worship a dead man, adore a cross on which he was crucified, and consider their own death to be glory and honour.'

Constantine went on, saying that he had chapels built for the martyrs, and destroyed the temples of the idols, honouring all who worshipped the true God and fought strenuously against other worships.

When the delegation returned to Armenia, Tiridates offered all the gold and silver gifts they had received to the service of the Church.

Gregory, having accomplished his mission, relinquished the care of the Church to his bishop son by appointing him as the next Catholicos in line of Armenia's Holy Apostolic Church. The aim of the new patriarch was to strengthen Christianity, not only in Armenia, but also in the Caucasus.

In the meantime, Tiridates continued to impose his new

Christian faith upon those in Armenia who still practised idol worship. As a result, armed conflicts ensued, between his forces and pockets of the resistance by the pagan priesthood. Thus, the king spent the rest of his life eliminating all ancient beliefs and destroying the remaining pagan idol temples and written documents. The temple of Garni, which had been erected for the king's sister Khosrovidukht, was converted into a royal summer residence.

Constantine the Great had initially moved the capital of the Roman Empire to the ancient city of Bosporus at Byzantium, where he legalized Christianity. In 324 AD, the city was renamed "New Rome", and the emperor declared it his new capital. The language and culture of his new seat of power were Latin. Theatrical pastimes of the late Roman Empire were introduced, and carnivals and spectacles, like chariot races, began to entertain the masses.

In 330 AD, Tiridates died, after failing in his attempt to centralize all power in Armenia. Rumours circulated that several members of the pagan nobility conspired against the king, and murdered him when out hunting. Tiridates' death was a cause for national mourning. His body was placed in a mounted coffin adorned with precious stones, ahead of which funeral songs were chanted by weeping women.

As for Gregory, he withdrew from active life to a sanctuary near Mount Sebuh, where he remained and lived as a hermit, with a small convent of monks, until his death in 331 AD.

From 336 AD, the Amatuni princes from the Armenian noble family were in charge of the tax administrative duties of the Armenian kingdom, when the fortress and possession of Oshakan – a major village in their royal domain – were bestowed upon them. In the same year, a battle took place near that village, between Armenians and Persians, which resulted in the crushing defeat of the latter. The political weight and military potential of this princely family was evident, from the feudal aid of 500 horses and cavalry soldiers they owed during the wars to their suzerain – the King of Armenia.

In 353 AD, Armenian nobles unanimously elected Prince Nerses as Catholicos (or Patriarch). A year later, he convened a council in Ashtishat, which was known as the First Armenian National-Ecclesiastical Council. The Council decided to build homes for the poor, as well as establishing orphanages, hospitals, and other caring institutions in different regions of Armenia. Moreover, they decided to establish monasteries, schools, and convents for women. The Patriarch Nerses succeeded in implementing these decisions – an achievement for which he later was called Nerses the Great.

Chapter 8

The Mamikonian family first appeared in the early fourth century, and came to be known as sparapets (hereditary grand marshals). The first known Mamikonid lord was Vatche Mamikonian. At the time of King Khosrov III Kotak, who served as a Roman Client King of Arsacid Armenia, and was the son of King Tiridates III, the Bznuni nakharars were military commanders and boundary governors. Their tribe householder, Databen Bznuni, disobeying the centripetal authorities, rebelled against the king. Vatche broke some of the rebels, but the rest escaped. After that, Databen was brought to the king in chains, accused of being a traitor, and condemned to death by stoning.

As manorial elite of Bznunis still existed, and that loyal house of patriarchal orders still retained the former disobedience of the centripetal authorities, Vatche was given a command to destroy their entire household, which was part of a conspiracy. Subsequently, the Bznuni possessions were confiscated and joined to the royal estates. Despite the elimination of the elite tribe, the dynasty of the Bznunis maintained their existence in feudal order. Vatche was eventually killed, during the Persian invasion of Armenia.

The Mamikonian family reappeared in 355 AD, when they were the greatest landholders, their lands including the province of Tayk in the north-west, and the region of Tarawn in the south-west. To these were subsequently added the patriarchal estates of Bagrevand, Daranalik, and Ekeleac, inherited by Prince Hamazasp Mamikonian through his marriage to Sahakanush, the daughter of the first Patriarch, Isaac. The family controlled vast sections of autonomous Armenian territories. The Mamikonians were a great family, and, through intermarriages to maintain bloodline between their patriarchs and their descendants, there was a unification of the most prominent feudal and ecclesiastical families in Armenia.

The office of sparapet belonged to the Mamikonian family, and it could not be alienated. When its holder was too young to perform his duties, a temporary surrogate replaced him. The Mamikonians also held another hereditary position, of royal tutor, and not even the ruler of Armenia had the power to deprive them of this office. Unable to be kings themselves, they instead played the role of kingmakers to the late enfeebled Armenian Arsacids.

Politically, the Mamikonian sparapets (Supreme Commanders) were viewed as the Hellenophile partisans of the Byzantine Empire, although the Armenian and Byzantine churches often differed on matters of dogma. Some of the Mamikonians had enjoyed patronage from the emperor in Constantinople for the honorary title of Prince of Armenia. Many of the sons of the former had served in the Byzantine army, and rose to the highest ranks. However, their loyalty to the Byzantines, and their hostility to Persia, were not unshakeable, as their political position wavered and on occasion reversed.

The family chief at the time was Vassak Mamikonian, the Armenian sparapet under the Roman client king, Arshak II, of Arsacid Armenia. The former, known to be a great general, won many victories against the Persian King Shapur II. In 367 AD, Vassak was eventually defeated through the treachery of Merujan Artsruni, who had earlier renounced Christianity, and moved to the Persian side for his Mazdian sympathies.

In 374 AD, Pap was placed on the throne, with Roman backing, but he was not popular with many of the nakharars, and the Armenian Church in particular, as he aggressively pursued a policy of Christian Arianism.

In the same year, when the Eastern Roman Emperor, Valens, interfered in Armenian affairs, King Pap became a victim of internal divisions and fighting between nakharars and Mushegh Mamikonian. The king was eventually killed, at the instigation of the emperor in the Roman camp, when informed that the former was veering towards an alliance with the Sasanians.

After the murder of Pap, Valens designated Varazdat as King of Arsacid Armenia, and had the office of sparapet bestowed on Vassak's son, Mushegh Mamikonian. A few years later, the king confirmed Mushegh as regent. But he soon feared the great influence Mushegh had gained within and outside of the country, as he claimed to have good relations with the Romans. The sparapet was even planning for a strategic partnership, to establish a common defence system between the two states. Posing a danger to his rule, and having played a part in Pap's murder, the king had Mushegh executed during a feast, at the behest of Sembat

Saharuni, who replaced him as the new sparapet. Mushegh's family put his body on a high tower, believing that the spirits would descend and bring him back to life, but it was all in vain.

In this complete political anarchy, the Mamikonids reacted to the assassination with dismay and indignation. They held an emergency meeting at their headquarters, to discuss the tragic events in Armenia, and especially the internal hurdles.

One of them said angrily, 'We've had enough of these treacheries to our family, and defections from the Artsruni camp.'

'I lamented over the death of Mushegh,' another Mamikonid said. 'I don't think he was posing a danger to Varazdat's rule.'

'I agree, he was wrongly accused of disloyalty to the Crown.'

'I think Mushegh's death was due to the false rumours spread by his councillor – Saharuni – and the king unscrupulously killed our brother for his so-called pro-Roman position.'

'That's right.'

'Valens must be aware of this execution.'

'Surely.'

'We need to appoint a new sparapet, to raise an insurrection against our common enemy.'

They all agreed with a nod.

After the murder of Mushegh in 378 AD, the victim's brother, Manuel Mamikonian, who had returned from Persian captivity, took his revenge on the traitor, Merujan Artsruni, for defecting to Persia and converting to

Zoroastrianism. He had him sadistically killed – a thin, circular, red-hot metal bar was placed around his head, instead of a crown.

Manuel then quickly raised a military force, and drove Varazdat and Saharuni out of Armenia. The former sought refuge in Rome, after four years of reign.

The new sparapet elevated Arshak III and his younger brother Vologases to the throne, as co-kings of Armenia. Afterwards, together with Zarmandukht, Queen consort of Armenia, he formed a provisional government allied with Persia, but in fact he aimed to place the country under Roman protection. Manuel treated the co-kings and the queen consort with honour during a short period of political stability in Armenia. As he soon discovered that the Persian ruler was plotting against him, he attacked and decimated his emissary's Suren army. Manuel continued to defend Armenian sovereignty until his death in 386 AD. Vologases also died in the same year, while Arshak, whose authority became incrementally reduced by the Sasanid invasions, fled to Western Armenia. This paved the way in the following year for the complete conquest of Eastern Armenia by the Persians.

PART TWO

Chapter 9

The year 387 AD marked the partition of Armenia between the Byzantine Empire and Sasanid Persia. The long-running disputes within the Armenian kingdom between the pro-Roman and pro-Persian nakharar clans accelerated this division. King Vramshapuh realized all the hardships in establishing relations with the aristocracy in his domain. In an attempt to maintain the integrity of the state, he abandoned dictatorial aspirations, and sought to form a government that would take into account the interests of the nobility. The king continued to rule over Eastern Armenia, and to maintain peaceful relations with both Persia and Byzantium. His reign was regarded as beneficent and illustrious.

Around 394 AD, Mesrop, leaving the Iranian court, became the royal scribe and imperial secretary for Vramshapuh. He prepared himself for a missionary life and holy service, but experienced great difficulty in spreading his message to common people. In fact, the books of the Bible were either in Greek or in Assyrian, and the liturgies were conducted in those languages for the population at that time. But the majority of the local Christians, except for a few highly educated individuals, could not understand or read Greek and Syriac scripts. Mesrop himself endeavoured to translate orally lections from the Scripture into a language more suitable for listeners during his preaching in the regions.

In order to master the nation's soul and conscience, the teacher thought it was invaluable for his people to be preached to in the Armenian language. He clearly realized this necessity when he was fighting against the remnants of Mazdaism in Goghtn. Moreover, the expropriation of two parts of Armenia – Eastern and Western – was threatening the unity of the nation. He consulted Daniel, an Assyrian pious bishop who claimed to have found the letters of the alphabet. Mesrop then set out to restore and rearrange the letters, but without success. For one thing, in the absence of vowels, the alphabet could not express the binding sounds of the ancient Armenian linguistics. As a result, it was forgotten for some time.

Given that Armenia's religious freedom was seriously threatened by Persian Mazdaism, King Vramshapuh and Isaac had the foresight to realize that unless Armenia segregated itself from its powerful neighbours, through intellectual development, its Christian nationality would perish. The king and the patriarch encouraged and prompted Mesrop to determine a national alphabet.

The teacher withdrew to a monastery, where he practised great austerities, enduring hunger and thirst. He slept on the ground, and spent many nights in prayer, and further studying the Holy Scriptures. He believed this piety was necessary to find a complete and accessible alphabet for his people, so that they could read the Bible, and thus he could save the nation from impending moral and physical destruction.

To help accomplish this difficult task, a Greek calligrapher named Rufinus was summoned to the monastery, where he assisted Mesrop in creating the Armenian alphabet. They both carefully reviewed the alphabets of Greek, Assyrian, Persian, and Aramaic, and the integrity of letters used for each language. The goal was to find how applicable all these alphabets were to the phonetic system of Armenian.

Mesrop finally concluded that Armenian phonetics were unique, and it was impossible to fully express them through any existing alphabet. He decided that his Armenian alphabet should consist of thirty-six symbols (twenty-eight consonants and eight vowels), corresponding to its phonetic composition. But this number did not yet include the vowels he was earnestly looking for. Later on, in a divine vision, the right hand of the Lord appeared before the eyes of his soul, and bestowed on him the missing vowel letters.

The discovery of the alphabet in 405 AD marked a symbolic time in Armenian history, leading to a prominent blossoming of Armenian literature. The first sentence written by Mesrop was the opening line of Solomon's Book of Proverbs, 1:2. "To know wisdom and instruction; to perceive the words of understanding."

Isaac and Mesrop set to work building the national spirit. Their aim was to separate the Armenians from other peoples of the East forever, and make of them a distinct nation. Their initiatives were approved by the Christian communities of Mesopotamia, and relations between the Armenian and Assyrian churches began to improve. Moreover, the patriarch and the teacher endeavoured to strengthen their people in the Christian faith, by rendering profane all the foreign alphabetic scripts, which had been employed for transcribing the books of the Mazdian and Zoroastrian followers. The preservation of the language and literature of Armenia was due to Mesrop's hard work. Otherwise, the Armenian people would have been absorbed by the Persians, and, like many other nations of the East, would have disappeared.

Encouraged by the patriarch and Vramshapuh, the latter providing funds and assistance to carry out educational missions, Mesrop established many schools in which the youth were taught the Armenian alphabet. He himself taught in Amaras monastery, located in what is now the Martuni region. In teaching the Armenians the new language, he allowed them to better understand Christianity. The teacher then decided to extend his activity, and with letters from Isaac he went to Constantinople, where he met the Emperor Theodosius the Younger, and Patriarch Atticus. After receiving permission from them to teach in other Armenian-owned territories, he quickly returned to Byzantine Armenia, where he founded schools and introduced the new script to his pupils.

Returning to Persian Armenia, Mesrop reported on his missions to the patriarch, and continued preaching in Caucasian Albania, and in those districts that had been annexed to the latter and to Georgia. His aim was to unify all the Armenians in that region through linguistic bonds.

Mesrop reflected deeply on the people of Medes, who had settled in the north-western portions of present-day Iran – an area known in the past as Media. King Vramshapuh was quite amazed at Mesrop's intention to further his Christian mission amongst these wild Median tribes. The teacher explained to the king that his real motive for undertaking this was to educate these heathen people about having godly wisdom, so that they could be eloquent speakers for future generations, and distinguishable from their compatriots. When the king asked if these uncivilized people could be educated, Mesrop replied positively. Permission was granted, and Mesrop successfully fulfilled his arduous mission and task.

While the architects of the Christian religion were Gregory the Illuminator and King Tiridates, the trio of Vramshapuh, Mesrop and Isaac nationalized Christianity. Vramshapuh was materially and morally the literacy project's great patron.

Chapter 10

Mesrop brought Sarkis' relics back from Assyria to Armenia, and St Sarkis Monastery was built over them, outside the village of Ushi. With sadness, Mesrop recalled the events that led up to the execution of the martyr-saint.

Back in 337 AD, the Roman Emperor Constantine the Great had appointed Sarkis, a Greek by birth but a Roman citizen, as general-in-chief of the Roman army stationed in Cappadocia. In one battle, with just forty soldiers Sarkis had defeated an enemy force of 10,000. He had also travelled from town to town, teaching the Gospel, and had churches built for the pagan followers. As a devout Christian, he always helped the poor, and punished the wicked.

When Constantine died, his pagan nephew, known as Julian the Apostate, succeeded him, and in 361 AD Julian took the throne. He made paganism the religion of the empire once more, and issued an edict that Christians should be banned from professing their faith. Thus, he ordered all churches be destroyed, and all Christians be persecuted and massacred – a harsh reaction against the Christianization of the Roman Empire by his uncle. The martyrs were bullied, their torturers trying in vain to force them into worshipping the ancient gods.

Sarkis was very concerned about these events, and prayed for a solution. An angel had appeared to him and said, 'It is time for you to leave your clan, as did Abraham the Patriarch, and go to the country which I will show you, where you will receive the crown of righteousness.'

Sarkis, leaving his military position, sought refuge in Armenia, with his son Mardiros, under the protection of King Tiran. The latter served as a Roman client king of Arsacid Armenia, whose reign had been blemished by internal and external conflicts. Tiran had antagonized the clergy, with whom he had many disagreements. He also had two leading nobles from the Artsruni and Rshduni dynasties killed, accusing them of having secret relations with the Sasanids.

It was during this period that Shapur II – also known as Shapur the Great – the son of Hormiz II, reigned over the Sasanian Empire. The Sasanians called their empire Eranshahr (the land of the Iranians). Shapur's reign saw the military resurgence of the country, and the expansion of its territory, which marked the start of the first Sasanian golden era. At a very young age, he had launched very successful military campaigns against Arab insurrections and tribes, who knew him as the monarch "who pierces shoulders".

Shapur pursued a harsh religious policy. Under his reign, the collection of the Avesta – the sacred texts of Zoroastrianism – was completed, heresy and apostasy were punished, and Christians were persecuted. Thus, he reacted against the Christianization of the Roman Empire by Constantine the Great.

Shapur was amicable towards Jews, who lived in relative

freedom, and gained many advantages during his time. However, he attempted to introduce Zoroastrian orthodoxy into Armenia, but the Armenian nobles, secretly supported by the Romans, successfully resisted him.

After crushing a rebellion in the south, Shapur invaded Roman Mesopotamia and southern Armenia, but was resisted by the valiant Roman defence of the fortress of Amida (now Diyarbakir, Turkey). The Romans finally surrendered, after a seventy-three-day siege, during which the Persian army suffered huge losses.

Shapur continued his operations against the Roman fortresses, capturing two, again at heavy cost. In late 361 AD, Constantius II, the son of Constantine the Great, who had elevated him to the imperial rank of Caesar, launched a counter-attack, having spent the winter in Constantinople, making considerable preparations.

Shapur, who had lost the aid of his Asiatic allies, avoided battle, but left strong garrisons in all the fortresses which he had captured. Constantius laid siege to one of those without success, and retired to Antioch on the approach of winter. He died soon after.

Meanwhile, Julian the Apostate was determined to avenge the Roman reverses in the east. Although Shapur attempted an honourable reconciliation, having been warned of the capabilities which Julian had displayed in wars against the Alemans in Gaul, the emperor dismissed any prospect of negotiation.

When the slaughtering of Christians by Julian's army continued in Antioch and Syria, Sarkis and his son left for the Sasanian Empire, on King Tiran's insistence. The latter was mainly concerned to appease Shapur, who had designs on Armenia, where he could count on support from some of its nobility. Shapur, having heard of Sarkis' reputation as a brave warrior and skilled military leader, had designated him as commander of the Persian army.

On his white steed, Sarkis headed towards Julian's forces of 65,000, assembled from Roman citizenry and tribes in the Germanic north. The clatter of Sarkis' galloping horse's hooves thundered over the ground, which shook as though hit by an earthquake. Snowstorms and blizzards raged, conducted by Sarkis' spear. As Julian advanced to Shapur's capital city of Ctesiphon in 363 AD, Sarkis quickly repulsed the enemy's forces, and heroically prevented their entry into the fortified city. Eventually, Julian realized that to take the city would take a long time, and he did not have the provisions to feed his troops. Withdrawing towards the north, he was killed during one of several cavalry skirmishes that plagued the Romans' retreat to their own territory.

During the early years of Shapur's reign, there was also a rise in persecution of his Christian subjects, partly due to the identification of their political leaders as agents of foreign enemies, but mostly due to the disobedience of the empire's religious leaders, who had failed adequately to fulfil the obligations imposed by the court on them. Known as the "cycle of martyr", instigated by some Persian elites, a large number of Christians had been put to death. But this violence was restricted to ecclesiastical leaders – bishops and priests – who had rejected an invitation to participate more actively in the administration of the empire. It was not a systematic persecution of common Christians as a collective. Among the martyrs were Shemon Sabbae, Patriarch of the Church of the East, and his clergy.

When word of the Christian faith of Sarkis and baptism reached Shapur, he summoned him, together with his son and the fourteen baptized soldiers, to his palace. With the intention of testing their faith, they were then escorted in the king's presence to a fire temple, to participate in a Zoroastrian ceremony, and to offer sacrifices there.

'I will worship only one God – the creator of Heaven and Earth,' Sarkis said bluntly.

'Why?' the king asked with disdain.

'Because fire and idols are not gods.'

As Sarkis rushed into the temple and destroyed all the objects there, the surrounding crowd fell upon him. 'How dare you destroy our gods!' they shouted at him.

Outraged by Sarkis' actions, the king ordered his soldiers angrily, 'Bring the son here, and have him killed before his father's eyes.'

Deeply distressed, Sarkis witnessed the scene of his son's murder, and the decapitation of his fourteen faithful companion soldiers as well.

Sarkis was imprisoned, and later the king ordered his execution, at which an angel descended from Heaven and told him, 'Be brave, do not fear the killers, for the gate of the Kingdom of Heaven is open for you.'

After he died, a mysterious light appeared over his body and then faded away. Sarkis' loyal Christian followers retrieved his body, and, wrapping it in a clean linen, sent it to Assyria.

Chapter 11

Yazdegerd I acceded to the Sasanian throne in 399 AD, and consolidated his power during the Golden Age of Armenian literature. He had succeeded his brother, Bahram IV, after the assassination of the latter in the same year. He was killed by an arrow during a hunting expedition. The nobility were to blame for the murder, which they had ordered because of his attempt to reduce the authority of the powerful Parthian noble families – known as wuzurgan – who formed the bulk of the Sasanian feudal army.

The new king, who was a Zoroastrian, but a peaceful ruler, started his reign with lenience and justice. His general good disposition towards the Persian citizens within his realm, and especially towards Rome, earned him the epithet "the most quiet". When the Romans were in a perilous state, as a result of armed revolt by the Black Sea Germanic groups in the eastern provinces, the king returned Roman captives whom the Persians had rescued after routing an invasion of the Huns.

Yazdegerd's good will was so well known that Emperor Arcadius entrusted him in his will with the guardianship of his infant son, Theodosius, to earnestly preserve the empire for the Roman prince.

When Arcadius died, the Persian monarch at once addressed a letter to the Senate of Constantinople, saying he accepted the charge, and threatened war if any should attempt to conspire against his ward. With absolute loyalty to the emperor's behest, he continued to defend the life, power, and possessions of Theodosius. The guardianship of the prince set the stage for implementing a policy of peace with the Romans, with mutual respect. Thus, Yazdegerd enjoyed cordial relations with the Eastern Roman Empire, and never went to war with them. His policy of peace towards the Romans earned him the praise of the Byzantines, who called him a king of noble character. During the reign of King Vramshapuh, his peaceful political activity had also won the confidence of the Persian king, as well as of the pro-Roman Armenians.

In the course of time, however, Yazdegerd misused his sharp intelligence and his versatile knowledge. At home, he showed stubbornness, great suspicion, and selfishness, treating others with contempt. As a volatile ruler, he harshly punished the slightest failure, and warned he would not tolerate any opposition to his will. He ignored any advice given in his court, except when it came from foreign envoys, and prevented those in his entourage from forming any close friendships with each other.

One day, he had summoned his ministers to the royal court, to make an important announcement: 'After much thought, and in view of the Christian persecutions in the past, I've decided to allow the country's non-Zoroastrian people – Christians and Jews alike – to practise their faith freely.'

Amazed, one of the ministers said, 'You're making a

grave error, Your Majesty. The nobility and priesthood will never approve of that.'

'I don't need your advice on what I have to do,' Yazdegerd said bluntly.

Another minister warned, 'Your new friendly relations with the religious minorities will create trouble and social unrest in your domains.'

'You'll be called a sinner for betraying your own faith, and humiliating the priesthood,' a third minister added.

Despite the ministers' warnings, the king was determined to proceed with his religious strategy, and issued several specific orders that Christians were not to be molested by the Magi. On the other hand, he warned that to convert any person from Zoroastrianism to Christianity was a crime punishable by death – a direct reference to teachers and disciples.

Bishop Marutha of Martyropolis, a city which he founded in Mesopotamia, was famed for his knowledge and his piety. He had acted as ambassador to the East Roman Emperor at Ctesiphon, and protected Persian Christians, while securing peace between the Eastern Roman Empire and Persia. Thus, by his affability and saintly life, he gained Yazdegerd's esteem and confidence. The king was also an ardent follower of Abdaas – the bishop of Ctesiphon.

On Marutha's advice, in 410 AD the king issued a decree termed "the Edict of Milan for the Assyrian Church". It permitted Christians to worship openly, and rebuild ruined churches, allowing bishops to travel freely in their dioceses. As a result, more churches, shrines to martyrs, and monasteries were built in prominent places across the empire. The king, together with Iranian church leaders, contributed funds towards such constructions, and increased the participation of secular Christians and Church elites in the Iranian administration. For the benefit of the Persian Church, Marutha held two synods at Ctesiphon, and convinced the king to convene a religious council in Seleucia, to organize all Church affairs. The bishop was reputed to be the author of numerous works on Christian history and theology.

On another occasion, the saintly bishop visited Yazdegerd's court again, and asked permission for transferring all the relics of Christian martyrs from Persian territory to Byzantium. As permission was granted, the bishop proceeded with his mission, and later had the bones deposited within the walls of the village of Martyropolis.

Yazdegerd acknowledged his friendly relations with the Jews, and the Christians of the Church of the East. His gestures of generosity and good will included not only permission for Christians to bury their dead, which Zoroastrian priests believed tainted the land, but also the authority for Christ to be openly praised, both in their lives and in their deaths. He gave both his Christian and Jewish subjects such freedom and support that the latter hailed him as a new Cyrus. Moreover, the king provided so well for the poor and the wretched that they prayed daily for the safety of the victorious and glorious king, whose good manners were a landmark in the history of the Christians.

But Yazdegerd's religious and peaceful policies were disliked by the nobility and Zoroastrian clergy, whose power and influence he strove to curb. Always eager to impose sovereign authority, the king was actually at odds with the members of his clergy and nobility. Well aware of the fate of his predecessors, Bahram IV and Shapur III, who had been deposed and killed by the Persian nobility, he could not put his trust in them any longer, and prevented them from acquiring excessive influence at the expense of royal power. However, the hostility of the priesthood towards the king increased, as he executed several priests, who disapproved of his friendly management of the religious minorities.

Chapter 12

After the death of Vramshapuh in 414 AD, Isaac visited the court of Yazdegerd, who consented with him releasing Khosrov IV from political exile. The latter reigned a second time, as his nephew, Artaxias IV, was too young to rule, but Khosrov died a year later. Artaxias was then appointed King of Armenia by the Sasanids.

The singular upsurge of Armenian literature would not have occurred if Yazdegerd had not pursued a policy of religious toleration by issuing a decree permitting Christians to worship openly, to rebuild ruined churches, and allowing bishops to travel freely in their dioceses. The Armenian clergy was even completely free to maintain contact with Constantinople. This patronage of Christianity outraged the Persian Magi when the king used the Catholicos twice as a mediator and envoy; first to Theodosius, and secondly to mediate between the king and his brother who governed Pars.

But Yazdegerd was soon disappointed that the bishop of the city of Hormizd-Ardashir, along with a group of Christian priests and laymen, had levelled a Zoroastrian fire temple. He immediately summoned them to his court for their actions and asked the bishop, 'Since you're the chief of these men, why do you allow them to despise our gods, to disobey our command, and to do their own free will?' After a pause, he went on angrily, 'Do you destroy our shrines of worship and the foundations of our fire temples, which we have received from our forefathers to honour?'

The bishop hesitated to answer, and a priest in his group replied, justifying his action, 'I've put out the fire, because it is not a house of our God. Demolishing a fire temple was just a way of showing the victory of Christianity.'

'And the end of the Zoroastrian faith?' the king asked in amazement and continued, 'You see, it is not fair to abolish one faith to the advantage of another. I order you now to have the fire temple rebuilt, and altars restored.'

The bishop refused the order, and when the priest extinguished the sacred fire of Zoroastrians, celebrating mass there, the two men were immediately executed.

Yazdegerd, in his very last year, yielding to pressure from the Zoroastrian priesthood, changed his policy towards his Christian subjects. He ordered a limited persecution and massacre of Christians in Sasanid-held territory, because, through boldness and missionary zeal, they had committed offensive acts, such as the destruction of fire temples, theft of property deeds, slandering of the Mazdian faith, and disobeying royal orders. Some Christians boldly confessed their faith in Christ, though many others sought to conceal it.

Persian officials fulfilled the king's orders, after which they destroyed newly erected churches. Yazdegerd's aim was to discipline the zealous Christians and aristocrats, rather than to target the common people, whose strong desire to practise their faith was cut short with bitter disappointment. Maharsapor, a noble Persian prince brought up as a Christian, was distinguished by his virtue, and by his zeal for Christian faith. He was also captured, along with two other religious men, the latter being submitted to various tortures by the order of an inhumane and vile magistrate – a man raised to that dignity from a slave, whose manners betrayed him as a sordid individual. But the prince was imprisoned for three years, and periodically tortured, while starved and forced to live amid inhumane conditions.

This term being elapsed, the same magistrate came to him and asked harshly, 'Do you still want to maintain your faith?'

'Absolutely,' Maharsapor replied firmly.

Since the prince remained defiant, the magistrate condemned him to be thrown into a dark pit, to perish there. Several days after this sentence had been executed, officers, under the orders of magistrate, opened up the pit shaft. To their astonishment, they found the prince, in divine light, on his knees with hands folded. As one of the officers shook him with a long stick and he fell down, they realized in surprise that the man had died in prayer.

Maharsapor thus triumphed over his enemies by such a death.

The oppression of both Zoroastrians and Christians within the Sasanid empire created profound discontent with the king's reign. The latter earned the epithet of the "wicked", and made several attempts to spread Zoroastrianism in Armenia.

In 420 AD, Yazdegerd had met his end in the remote

northeast region of Hyrcania, at the hands of his nobles. To cover the assassination, they created a myth that the king, while staying there, was killed by a fabulous white horse – an angel sent by God – which had emerged from a spring to end his tyranny, before returning to disappear back into the spring. Others believed that the king was more likely to have died of sickness than as a victim of conspiracy. The magnates sought to prevent the king's sons from ascending to the throne. His oldest son, Shapur, who served as the governor of Armenia, was assassinated as he marched to Ctesiphon to claim his rightful place. Another son of Yazdegerd, Bahram V, having the support of the Arab king of Al-Hirah – a Sasanian vassal – and also of Mihr Narseh, who was retained in office as chief minister, eventually gained the throne.

In 424 AD, the Persian Church proclaimed its full independence from the Roman Church, to ward off allegations of any foreign allegiance. The separation of churches was seen as a political (rather than theological) move. In an attempt to prevent renewed persecution, Christians of Persia embraced the Nestorian Creed, which denied the reality of Incarnation and represented Christ as a God-inspired man, rather than as God-made-man.

The Church of the East, as the national church of the Sasanian Empire, was headed by the Patriarch of the East seated in Seleucia-Ctesiphon, who continued a line that stretched back to the Apostolic age. The Church of the East was established by Thomas the Apostle in the first century, and its liturgical rite was the East Syrian that employed the Divine Liturgy of Saints Addai and Mari.

The Church of the East shared communion with those of the Roman Empire until the Council of Ephesus condemned Nestorius seven years later. As a result, his supporters took refuge in Sasanian Persia, where the Church refused accusations of Nestorianism. Taken as a heresy attributed to Nestorius, it was thereafter called the Nestorian Church by all the other Eastern churches, both Chalcedonian and non-Chalcedonian, and by the Western Church. In fact, the war between the Persian and Roman Empires had forced the Church of the East to distance itself from the Roman Church.

Chapter 13

In 428 AD, the Arsacid dynasty of Armenia was completely abolished by the Sasanids, in accord with some Armenian dynasts, and the territory was transformed into a province within Persia, known as Persian Armenia.

In fact, the abolition of the Arsacid dynasty was brought about by the Armenian princes, who had never regarded their king as preponderant, and had become increasingly opposed to that primacy.

However, the lack of a king put the Armenians in a state of anarchic independence.

Vahan Amatuni was appointed by the Persian king as assistant governor of Armenia. This left the Artsrunis quite safe from a distant control exercised by Persia and Byzantium. In the perennial struggle between these two major powers over Armenia, the Artsrunis tended, partly out of opposition to the Roman crown and partly due to the geographical position of their state, to occasionally adopt a pro-Persian policy.

Following the downfall of the Arsacids, the Kamsarakan princes also acquired considerable political power, due to their quasi-hereditary titles and important border lords on the northern frontier of their realm. The feudal aid they were expected to render to their suzerain – the King of Armenia – was fixed at nearly 600 horses.

During this period, the marzbans were installed, and endowed with considerable powers and prerogatives in the region over which they ruled. Although they had full civilian and military authority under Sasanian rule, they could not interfere with the privileges of the Armenian nobility. The marzbans were foreign to the latter in both language and race, and only occasionally were Armenians of proven loyalty appointed to these high posts. In campaigns, the marzbans usually engaged Armenian soldiers, and in cases of emergency could have troops brought from Persia. The Armenian pro-Roman nakharars were merely required to provide soldiers on request. In return, they received their royal insignia.

The Armenian king preserved some privileges at the Sasanian court, as a result of an ancient custom from the Parthian period. When an Armenian cavalry under its general came to the Sasanian residence, it was received by a delegate of the king, who inquired about the situation in Armenia before presenting it to the court.

The Armenian society was divided into three estates at the time: the nakharars, who had legal rights to maintain hereditarily owned territories/state positions/military power in their relations with the king; the magnates (lesser nobility), and a third estate formed by the merchants, peasants and farmers. Armenia was highly aristocratic, its peculiar feature being the Azat class (middle and lower nobility). They were a group of dynastic princes, descendants and successors of the earliest tribal chiefs, who considered themselves minor kings, and the King of Armenia *primus inter pares*. In time, feudalism was introduced, reaching its fullest development in the Arsacid period.

After the Ecumenical Council of Ephesus in 431 AD, Isaac wrote critical letters against various sects. He also wrote letters to the Byzantine emperor Theodosius II, the Patriarch of Constantinople, and Byzantine governor, in which he and Mesrop presented the Orthodox position of the Armenian Church.

In the following year, Vardan Mamikonian, from the village of Artashat (Artaxata), became a promising soldier, instead of entering the priesthood as others in his family had done. He was the son of Hamazasp Mamikonian, and the grandson of Isaac, who in turn descended from Nerses the Great, who had been elected Patriarch by the Armenian nobility back in 353 AD. There was a long family lineage traceable to an association of saints and dynasts. Vardan was considered the worthy representative and head of the Mamikonian family, which held the fifth position in the royal succession of Armenian kings. A member of Armenia's highest calibre aristocrats, the Roman Emperor Theodosius II and the Persian King Bahram V both conferred the rank of general upon Vardan. As the supreme commander of the Armenian forces within the Persian imperial army in 432 AD, and with a record of service in many engagements, he won laurels in military campaigns in Khorasan.

Equally important as Vardan's dedication to being a good commander was his dedication to being a faithful Christian, believing that one could not serve one's people without serving Christ at the same time. After each meeting with his ministers, Vardan read them a selection of Bible verses in Greek, to lift their spirits, and to help gain a new perspective on a difficult situation.

Chapter 14

The first monumental task of Armenian literature was the version of the Holy Scriptures. Isaac had previously made a translation of the Bible from the Syriac text, but this work had turned out to be imperfect. In late 432 AD, under Mesrop's and Isaac's joint auspices, disciples were sent – some to Edessa, Athens and Antioch; others to Alexandria and Constantinople – to master the languages necessary for translating the Bible into Armenian. The most prominent pupils were John of Egheghiatz, Joseph of Baghin, Yeghishe, and Moses of Khoren (Movses Khorenatsi). The first two scholars, having journeyed as far as Constantinople, brought back with them authentic copies of the Greek text. Moreover, many liturgical books, canons of church councils, and patristic texts were rendered into Armenian, together with the decrees of the first three councils – Nicaea, Constantinople, Ephesus – and the national liturgy written in Syriac.

In addition to other copies of the Scriptures, which were obtained later from Alexandria, Mesrop and Isaac and their assistants had translated the Greek version of the Bible according to its Old Testament and Origen's Hexapla. This version, intended to be used in the Armenian Church, was finally completed successfully, and published circa 434 AD. With a translation of the first Armenian Bible through the use of its own alphabet, a golden era of classical Armenian literature began, and this enlightening work was carried out in Persian Armenia. Mesrop, who had preached the Gospel in the earlier years, evangelized the people in many districts, as well as the Georgians and Albanians, adapting his alphabet to their language.

Movses, from the village of Khorena, who had learned oratory, theology and philosophy, also returned to Armenia in 439 AD, after seven years of study in Alexandria, Edessa and Byzantium. As he became an expert in Greek culture and language, he did not hesitate to call all Greece the mother of the sciences. It was about this time that Yeghishe, one of Mesrop's pupils, entered into military service, and then became the personal temporary secretary to the sparapet Vardan Mamikonian.

However, the pupils' return from abroad was viewed by the populace with a certain contempt. In fact, Persian policy lay at fault, as its rulers could not tolerate highly educated scholars fresh from Greek centres of learning, and this resulted in some persecution by the Persians. When Movses learned that his two religious masters – Mesrop and Isaac – had died in the same year, he lamented and reflected over their death. While the Armenians had awaited the students' return to celebrate their accomplishments, he had hastened from Byzantium, in the hope of joining the celebration. Instead, he found himself grieving at the foot of his teachers' graves... he did not even arrive in time to see their eyes close, nor to hear them utter their final words. At the initiative of the Amatuni princes, Mesrop was buried in Oshakan, while Isaac's body was taken to Taron, and buried in the village of Ashtishat.

Given this hostile atmosphere, Movses went into hiding in a village near Vagharshapat, where he endured poverty and destitution for some time, and lived in seclusion.

Gyut, the Armenian Catholicos, who was travelling through the area, happened upon Movses. Unaware of his identity, the spiritual leader invited him to supper, along with several of his students. Through a speech made by Movses there, they discovered that the Catholicos and he were once classmates. The two embraced and, as both were Chalcedonian Christians, Movses was removed from seclusion and appointed as bishop in Bagavan.

A prince by the name of Sahak Pakraduni paid the new bishop a visit. Having heard Movses' reputation, he had a brief, intimate talk with him about his health and daily life, after which he kindly suggested, 'Perhaps you can write a book on the history of Armenia.'

Struck by the good grace of the prince, Movses, delighted, said, 'Your request is eminently suited to my interests, and especially to my scholarly career.'

Sahak reminded him gently, 'The idea is to present the history of the Armenian nation in a systematic way, from the beginning up to the fifth century, with scientific objectivity, and truthfulness of facts.'

'Of course!' Movses replied. 'You see, even though we're a small nation, and have been conquered many times by enemy forces, yet many acts of bravery have been performed in our land, worthy of being written about and remembered. But alas, no one has bothered to write them down up to now.'

'I assume that's why you want to take up the work.'

Movses nodded and continued, 'It's really a shame that none of the nobles and princes in Armenia have cared to ask those wise men under their authority to write our history, or thought of bringing them in from outside.'

'You're right.'

'I would do my best to accomplish this work, and leave it as an immortal historic monument to you and future descendants.'

'Thank you, I'm so honoured to hear that.'

Prince Sahak left, wishing the bishop the best of luck.

Movses gave the whole work considerable thought, and decided to divide the book into three successive parts. Book I would include the legendary times of Hayk Nahabet (the founder of the Armenian nation) within the Biblical tradition; Book II would extend from the foundation of the Armenian kingdom and the Hellenistic period to the conversion to Christianity of King Tiridates III by St Gregory the Illuminator. Book III would cover the Arsacid/Parthian period of the fourth century to the fall of the native Arsacid dynasty in 428 AD.

The author's main aim was to draw on a chronological, coherent and analytical approach, for he believed there was no true history without chronology. As a meticulous antiquarian, he thought he should have access to old Persian historical sources at his disposal. However, considering these Iranian religious traditions – fables, folk tales and paganism – redundant, with mythical personages of the past later deified, he had to rely mostly on current contemporary legends, oral traditions, epic poems, Holy Scriptures, and early temple stories. It was imperative for him to write about the struggle between Rome and Persia over the control of Armenia, and its gradual domination by the late Sasanians, likewise tacitly acknowledging the secular jurisdiction of their rulers over the Armenian Church. Thus, he would cover the transfer of power from the Parthians to the Sasanians, revealing the apparent origin of both dynasties, as well as the Parthian origin of the local Armenian ruling House.

In the Third Book, Movses also wanted to describe how influential and powerful families, like the nobility and the Mamikonians, dominated the political, civilian, and military spheres of Armenia, based on the feudal fiefdoms each family ruled. He intended to commonly use the title of Marzban as a governor or viceroy, and that of Sparapet, corresponding to the commander-in-chief of the army.

Chapter 15

In 438/439 AD, matters came to a head with the succession of the new Sasanian king, Yazdegerd II, and his reappointed chief minister, Mihr Narseh, who kept the honorary title of Grand Vizier – the highest rank in the administrative hierarchy of the Sasanian empire. Although both were intransigent upholders of Mazdaism, the king, according to the ancient Armenian people, was a mixture of contrasting emotions. Sometimes "an arrogant, stubborn, enraged man", at other times "a moderate man of prompt disposition". As for his minister, he was a "powerful, sinister man", whose intentions differed from those of the king because of his Zurvanite belief.

Upon ascending the throne, Yazdegerd had numerous Zoroastrian fire temples erected across his dominion, and promoted the Mazdian religion, in the hope of gaining the support of his Christian subjects. He then went to war with the Eastern Roman Empire, with little success for either side. The Romans, in difficulties on their southern front, appealed for a quick end to war in return for payments to the Sasanids to defend the Caucasus. Yazdegerd and

Emperor Theodosius I made an agreement that no new frontier fortresses were to be built in Mesopotamia.

The king had meanwhile been fighting an uninterrupted war with the Kidarites – related to Huns – in his empire's northern and north-eastern provinces. But he suffered several defeats at the hands of the enemy, who attempted to force him to pay them tribute, which he refused, to avoid humiliation. He put the blame on the Christians, due to much of his cavalry consisting of Armenians and Iberians. Limited persecutions started with the Christian nobles of Karkh in Mesopotamia, followed by the target of the aristocracy of Iberia and Armenia, along with Zoroastrian aristocrats. He removed from the latter their advantage of entry to the court, and castrated men in his armies to generate eunuchs more dutiful to him than to their own families. These repressive measures were enacted mostly against the Christians in the Sasanian Empire, including their expulsion from the army. At the same time, the king sent Narseh to Armenia to impose Zoroastrianism on the members of the Armenian noble Houses.

Yazdegerd had originally continued his father's policy of appeasing the provincial magnates, but he turned away from them, and created a policy of his own. When the magnates told him that his new policy had offended the people, he said, 'It's wrong to presume that the ways in which my father behaved towards you, keeping you close to him, and bestowing upon you all that bounty, are binding upon all the kings that come after him… each age has its own customs.'

The Sasanid rulers had long been suspicious of Armenian Christians, and later of the Mamikonids clan. The former were viewed as spies, the latter as partisans, of Byzantium in Persian territory. Yazdegerd was concerned that the Armenian Church was hierarchically dependent on the Latin/Greek-speaking Orthodox Christian Church, aligned with Rome and Constantinople. He expected the Armenians to back the Aramaic-speaking Persian Church of the East, and tried to compel the Armenian Church to abandon the interests of Rome and Byzantium, or simply convert to Zoroastrianism. Yazdegerd's main aim was to banish all forms of Roman influence within his sphere of control, and to outlaw the studying of Greek culture – both the speaking and translation of Greek. In fact, he feared that Christianization would strengthen Armenia's links with the Roman empire, and set back the Persian cultural influence.

To cut the bonds of friendship with the Byzantine Emperor Theodosius II, and bind the Armenians to Iran, the king invaded the Byzantine territories of Mesopotamia, where he destroyed cities, burned churches, and seized captives. The emperor, unable to recapture his lost lands, concluded a humiliating peace in 441 AD, which, among other terms, stipulated that those Persian Christians who had taken refuge in the Byzantine domain must be surrendered. Yazdegerd then increased the fiscal obligations on the Church, as a means of pressure, and appointed more Persian-friendly bishops. A delegation of nobles and clergy invited to Persia was even forced to convert to the Persian religion, on pain of death.

To put an end to activities endangering the newly established Armenian Church, a council was convened by Catholicos Hovsep I in Shahapivan, on June 24th, 444 AD. It was attended by a delegation of political and religious figures of the nation, including Vasak Siuni, Vardan Mamikonian, and priest Ghevont Yerets. The latter, having studied under Mesrop and Isaac, was imbued with patriotism, nationalism, and religious devotion. The delegation compiled for their society a number of rules that covered marriages, laws and regulations regarding clergy and celibacy.

It was sometime during this earlier period, following the death of Veh Mihr Shapur, that Yazdegerd appointed Vasak as the lord of the province of Siunik (southern region of Armenia). The Siunia had been a notable family of ancient Armenian nobles – the first dynasty to rule as nakharars over this province.

Their first ruler was Valinak Siak, who was succeeded by his brother Andok. Back in 379 AD, Babik, the son of Andok, was re-established as a nakharar by the Mamikonian family, but his rule lasted for less than ten years. Since then, the Siunia family had fully integrated into the feudal aristocracy of the country, and managed their affairs as a virtually autonomous principality.

Artak Rshtuni was a member of the old Armenian noble House of Rshtuni, which appeared back in about 330 AD and ruled the region of Rshdunig – a canton of the province of Vaspurakan of historical Armenia. The first attested member of the house was Manadjihr Rshtuni. It was during that period that he and another member of the same house revolted against the King of Armenia, Tiran, who ordered the execution of their families. After Artak was attested in 445 AD, the Rshtuni family continued to rule from their region, and for the most part supported the Sasanid Persians against the Byzantines.

Chapter 16

A more acute danger faced Armenians, when Yazdegerd observed them to be the most zealous in the worship of God; especially those who belonged to the nakharar families and had adhered to the holy teachings of the apostles. The king beguiled some of them with gold and silver; others with posts of authority, all with false promises. Eventually, the king was persuaded by his chief minister, Narseh, to take firm steps against the Persian empire's Christian subjects – an attempt to re-impose Zurvanite Zoroastrianism on an already Christian Armenia. In fact, the Sasanians were well aware that the Armenians had been Zoroastrians before they converted to Christianity. Although the majority of Christians and their churches considered Zurvanism heresy and opposed to Zoroastrianism, some of the locals were completely unaware of its Zurvanite doctrine.

A royal edict, promulgated in 449 AD, required the Armenians and other Caucasian countries to renounce Christianity and perform Mazdian rites. The edict also prohibited the Jewish communities of the empire from celebrating the Sabbath in public, and ordered them to shut down their schools. Moreover, idols and idolaters had to be destroyed, to make way for Zoroastrian shrines. Thus, all these peoples had to render homage to the fire, and fulfil the ordinance of the magi, without omitting any detail. Yazdegerd declared at the royal court: 'Persecution of Christians, Jews, or others, is not necessarily an important feature of my project, nor was it of my predecessor. But I want to warn all of my non-Zoroastrian subjects not to challenge the supremacy of the Zoroastrian Religion through disobedience to the King of Kings.'

The king's active policy was actually to bring the whole of the non-Zoroastrian population in line with the state religion of Zoroastrianism. It was to create a uniform religious identity among his subjects, as part of his centralization programme. As they all roundly condemned the tough arbitrary commands, Yazdegerd ordered executions of a few Jewish leaders. The people of Isfahan retaliated by lashing and killing two Zoroastrian priests. This incident caused the king to apply harder measures against the Jews, who were actually expecting the coming of the Messiah, which coincided with the fifth century AD.

After that, the king sent a threatening directive letter, through his chief minister, to Armenian notables. Before setting forth the precepts of the Persian religion, he wrote: 'Every man who dwells beneath the heavens and holds not to the Mazdian religion is deaf and blind, and is deceived by Ahriman. Therefore, there are two options for you now; either you answer this letter fully, or you shall come to my court to present yourselves to the Great Council.'

In response to the king's directive letter, an important meeting was held in the city of Artashat, where bishops, high-ranking clergy, and leading princes from all districts and provinces assembled. Catholicos Hovsep presided over the national assembly, whose spokesman was priest Ghevont. In the response letter, they set forth an elucidation of the Christian faith: 'The hands that had created Heaven and Earth are the same ones which carved on tablets of stone and gave us a Scripture, wherein the laws of peace and redemption are contained, so that we acknowledge the one only God.

'We discredit the concept of the Persian religion of two separate gods, that of good and that of evil. One country cannot have two rulers, nor can one creature have two gods. Should two kings venture to rule over one country, the latter would be destroyed, and the kingdom would cease to exist.

'No one can shake us from our faith, neither sword nor fire, or all other horrid tortures. Our religion is not like a garment that we can change according to the circumstances; it is part of our bones and blood. We've served you loyally in your army, and always paid you taxes. If you leave us to our belief, we will here on earth choose no other master in your place. But we need to obey our Lord, who is the Lord of Lords and the King of Kings eternally.

'Should you force your will upon us or require anything beyond this great testimony, our bodies are in your hands; do with them as you please. We are no better than our forefathers, who had surrendered their possessions and their bodies for the sake of this faith. We are ready to die for the love of Christ, who took death on himself so that we, by his death, might be freed from eternal death and thus be made participants in immortality.

'We do not wish to be interrogated further, for our covenant to be faithful is not with man but with the Almighty God, from whom nothing can separate us, neither now, nor later, nor forever and ever.'

The letter was signed by all the attendees in the national assembly, and, remaining faithful to their vows, it was sent to the royal court.

Chapter 17

Yazdegerd felt very disparaged when he received the response letter from the Armenian national assembly, and read their rejection of his demands. He issued a harshly worded order to summon the chief dignitaries of Armenia to his court. On the Saturday before Easter Sunday, fifteen nobles, headed by Vardan and Vasak Siuni, arrived at the royal court in Ctesiphon.

The king, who put aside common courtesies such as heralding the guests with military honours, as was the usual custom, received them rather rudely. He bellowed and said, 'I've sworn by the great sun god, which illumines the whole world by its rays, giving life to all creatures on earth, that if tomorrow morning at its magnificent rise you don't kneel before it with me, and acknowledge it as our god, I will not spare you, and will bring upon you all manner of persecutions and tortures, until you shall carry out my commands.'

One of the nakharars gently reminded the king, 'We've always performed our military services, proclaimed our loyalty to you, and have paid the substantial taxes, all of which have been even more and greater during your reign than at any other time.'

'Since you're all subjects of my empire, it is your duty to serve me. And I want to make it clear that nobody shall have close ties to Byzantium, with its Orthodox Christian Church. Such links would only create uprisings in my territory.'

The pro-Roman Armenian nobles felt pressured to cooperate with the Sasanid Empire against Byzantium.

'I reiterate for the last time that I want all of you to renounce Christianity, and shift back to Mazdaism,' the king said bluntly.

Vasak realized that his authority as a Christian viceroy of Persian Armenia was undermined by the king's religious policy of imposing Zoroastrianism.

But Vardan spoke up fearlessly: 'The convictions of Christianity I had studied at an early age were truths. I could not disavow them, preferring even to die than to deny those truths.'

The king writhed at Vardan's words and retorted, 'Stop telling me absurdities, you must obey my orders at all costs.'

'You mean you'd like us to rebuild fire temples and altars?' a nakharar asked in amazement.

'Exactly,' the king said harshly.

As they all remained silent for a while, Yazdegerd realized they were unlikely to agree to his irrevocable demands. He issued an order of imprisonment, thinking that this could change their mind, and continued in a threatening tone, 'You cannot cancel out my strong conviction, and I won't let you have your wish so easily. I will banish all of you, and send into your country numerous forces, with elephants, and will have your wives and children deported forcefully to the far south of my domains. I will also destroy your churches and so-called shrines, and should any man oppose my will, he shall be subjected to a merciless death.'

The Armenian nobles were taken to prison, at the back of which they knelt in prayer, and murmured their firm declarations of faith. In the evening, one of the king's advisors – a secret Christian himself – who sensed a great tragedy was threatening the prisoners and their people, came to them. 'I'm a Christian like yourselves,' he murmured. 'Your only chance to be released from prison is to feign renunciation of your faith.'

The nobles exchanged a look, taking the man's proposal into serious consideration, except for Vardan, who said firmly, 'I will not feign my faith, in whatever way.'

In an attempt to persuade him to fake his conversion, one of the nobles said gently, 'We have no choice but to pretend a temporary renunciation.'

Another noble interposed, begging Vardan, 'Please, for the sake of our homes and families, we have to prevent them from suffering a worse fate.'

They all stared anxiously at Vardan, waiting for a reply. After a moment of deep reflection, he reluctantly agreed.

They quickly sent word to the king, saying they had yielded, to show outward respect for certain practices of the Persian religion, such as bowing to the sun.

The king, not entirely convinced of the nobles' renunciation of their faith, hoped nevertheless that they would carry out his commands. This was part of a clever conspiracy to leave Armenia without leadership, and thus facilitate the conversion of the common people to Zoroastrianism. Moreover, he believed that with the help of the Armenian warriors, he could defeat the Kushans, who had beaten his army and left many regions in ruin.

Chapter 18

The Armenian chief dignitaries were released from prison and sent back to Armenia in the company of 700 Magians, who had received precise orders from the king, to impose strict observance of various Mazdian practices. They were to close the churches and turn them into fire temples, forcibly secularize the monks and nuns by making them wear lay costume, compel the wives of the satraps and the children of Armenians to receive instructions in the doctrines of Zoroaster, suppress marriage laws and establish polygamy, and to have esculent animals slaughtered and sacrificed to the gods. It was unimaginable to force these shocking practices upon a people who had officially adopted Christianity for over 140 years. Hardly had the cavalcade crossed the frontier when a horde of armed Armenian peasants led by priest Ghevont assailed the trespassers, and sent them fleeing.

In the meantime, the local people, having heard of the faithlessness of their nobles, and not realizing they had merely feigned the renunciation of their religion, felt they had dishonoured themselves in the eyes of the many other

Christian natives. Furious and indignant, the Armenians, under the leadership of a military noble, decided to avenge themselves on their traitorous kin.

However, Vardan, along with fifteen nobles, finally joined his people to fight for Christianity to the very end. His partisans had first captured one of the Armenian magnates for having built temples at Artaxata. When the chief of the Magians and his men tried to break down the doors of the church, the people, armed with clubs and cudgels, attacked them, and forced them back to their camp. Vasak, who witnessed these attacks in shock, feared to speak out. His two sons had been taken hostage to the court of Ctesiphon, and his son-in-law, Varaz, had fled to the Persian capital.

Yazdegerd discovered that the Armenian nobles had betrayed him as they chased back the group of Persians who had accompanied them. Moreover, he learned that the local people had revolted against the Magians, who were ill-received almost everywhere, and in some cases massacred. The Armenian ruler was directly replaced by Narseh, who took control of Armenia with the assistance of the chief priest. Narseh was called a sinister, embittered man, and a snake.

Vardan strongly repudiated the Persian religion, and in 448-49 AD took the lead in the Armenian rebellion against the Sasanian overlords. Priest Ghevont, together with a number of bishops, roused the people with a cry for resistance against the Magi. The Kamsarakans, under Arshavir II – an Armenian prince from the family – and Vahan Amatuni, also took part in the revolt, to protest the king's attempt to impose the Zoroastrian religion. As a result, Vahan and several other dynasts of the Armenian

Houses were expelled to Gorgan, northeast of Persia.

For the love of power and of the throne of Armenia, a faction of Armenians, led by Prince Vasak Siuni, cast off their pretence of patriotism, and allied themselves with the Sasanians against the rebellion. Vasak committed acts of vengeance: he destroyed churches, imprisoned priests, and arrested members of the Mamikonian and Kamsarakan nobility, to be taken to the Persian capital as hostages.

Vardan, who was quickly informed of Vasak's betrayal, hurried home from a long journey of 400 miles. Enraged, he led his mounted knights out to avenge the defectors, who had fled into the heights of the Siunik Mountains. The Armenian commander soon blockaded the renegade armed forces, while Vasak looked for a way out, and, in a desperate attempt, managed to escape. Vardan shouted at him, 'You traitor! You will be tried for treason. Come back and fight against me if you have the guts!'

The commander gave up his pursuit of the foe fugitive as he disappeared from view. Vasak, also acting as an adviser to the Persian commander, was in contact with the allied nations of the Caucasus, and the dominant princes of the border provinces, subtly trying to discredit the rebellion movement. The traitor then presented himself as a mediator, calling for cessation of domestic armed conflict, and of all anti-Sasanian activities. But he failed in his mediation, for he was hated by his compatriots for alleged Mazdian sympathies. Despite his cowardly, treacherous defection, the rebellion movement cut across class lines, and had the full support of the bulk of the nobility, the Church, and the common people as well. Eventually, several important cities, including Artagert and Garni, were recaptured by the rebels. The chief of the Magians pleaded for his life, and promised he would write to the Persian king, to abandon the plan of converting the Armenians to fire-worshipping. They did not believe him, and had the chief and his son executed.

This provided a justification for Yazdegerd to declare war on Armenia. He ordered Narseh to summon the generals, and bring forward the company of elephants. Narseh did so, and then put one of his top generals, Mushkan Nusalavurd, in charge of organizing the Persian army. The supreme commander divided the elephants into groups, assigning to each animal between 1000 and 2000 armed men. The elephants, equipped with clad towers, contained a contingent of bowmen, and because of the shock effect due to their size, were used as weapons in Persian wars, as well as command posts for senior officials to break through on the battlefield. Members of the elite fighting units were trained in personal battle style.

Chapter 19

On May 26, 451 AD, in springtime and in the predawn darkness, a massive Sasanid army, led by Mushkan, marched towards Armenia from Atropatene, accompanied by many armoured war elephants. Arriving in Zarevand, where they joined with Vasak Siuni's forces, the Persian army laid out a camp, defended by bastions and moats.

As the light of the dawn slowly unwrapped the darkness, Vardan was quickly informed of the encampment of the Persian troops. He called in one of his officers and said, 'I want you to send out our scouts, to survey the enemy's position, strength, and movements.'

Arriving at the Persian camp, the soldiers had a brief brush with the rear guard and, after vanquishing it, returned jubilant to their own camp. After being informed of the survey, Vardan declared to his troops, 'The Persians greatly outnumber our army, and are well equipped with their hordes of elephants. But keep your faith in Christ, for He is on our side.'

During this year, the Armenians, in preparation for the upcoming battle of Avarayr, were unable to send their church delegation to the Council of Chalcedon, to give their resolute adherence to the doctrine of monophysitism, and to reject the duophysitism of the Roman Church.

Vardan sent an emissary to Constantinople and appealed for aid, as he had good personal relations with Theodosius II, who had made him a general. The emperor agreed to help, but he unexpectedly died before he could take any action. His successor, the Emperor Marcian, counselled by diplomats, quickly adopted an opposite policy, concluding a peace with the Persian king, and assuring him of the absolute neutrality of the Byzantine government in regional conflicts – so there was to be no military assistance for the Armenians.

The disappointing news aroused among the Armenians feelings of hatred and detest for the Byzantines. With no reinforcements coming, Vasak Siuni and his partisans saw another reason to remain faithful to their Persian suzerain.

Vardan and his officers realized the gravity of the situation. In response to a comment made by his advisor, priest Ghevont, that the Armenian troops may lack military equipment over time, the commander replied firmly that they had to go to war with what they had, and not to be too concerned about resources. Also, they had to accept the challenge, put their trust in God, and prefer honourable death to dependency on others for aid.

The day before the battle, the Armenian volunteer forces led by Vardan camped for the evening near the village of Avarayr in north-eastern Iran. The mounted military leader, with his knights standing in red armour on each side of his horse, delivered a rousing battle speech to his troops. 'You and I have been in many battles together. In some, we triumphed gallantly, over the Huns and Turkic tribes; in others, the enemy defeated us. But our victories have been greater in number than our defeats. All these, however, were only for some personal glory, because we were fighting at the command of a temporal mortal king. He who deserted was called a coward throughout the land, and put to death, whereas he who pressed onward valiantly gained fame for bravery, and received splendid gifts from that king.'

Vardan vividly recalled how he had served mortal lords in his battles. 'We all have numerous scars and wounds on our bodies, but I consider all the honours received for our great courage useless, because they will all fade away sooner or later. Now then, if we were able to perform such brave deeds in obedience to a mortal king, how much more should we do for our Immortal King – the Lord of the living and dead.

'Since you have selected me as your supreme commander, let my words be agreeable to you all. Fear not the enemy, and never turn your backs to their frightful swords, because should our Lord grant us victory, we shall destroy their might, and the cause of righteousness shall be blessed. But if the time has come for us to meet a holy death in this upcoming battle, let us then accept our fate with joyful heart, without mingling cowardice with our valour and courage.

'I shall never forget the time when some of us, including myself, deceived the wicked ruler and misled him like a child, feigning to accede to his impious will, but the Lord bore witness to the fact that within our hearts we remained totally bound to Him. As you yourselves know very well, for the sake of our dear ones, who were in great distress, we sought all means to secure their lives, and together with them struggled against the enemy for the preservation of the God-given laws of our land.

'We all remember some engagements in which divine intervention enabled us to crush the royal armies of the Majus, and to obliterate the blasphemous idolatry practised by the king. In fact, we put on Christianity like a garment, and as man cannot change the colour of the skin, so he cannot and will never succeed in changing our minds. We believe the foundations of Christianity are firmly set on an immovable rock, not only on this earth, but in Heaven above.'

For a few moments, Vardan had a vision of Jesus, with a light around the back of His head. The commander then continued his speech, 'Gallant warriors! Like all Christians, we have the distinction of being God's chosen people. Knowing this, brothers, I assure you the Lord works for the good of all of those who remain steadfast in their faith. If by destroying others for the sake of divine laws we were able to gain fame and glory, how much more valuable will be the reward were we to die for the great testimony of our Lord Jesus Christ!

'This assertion is appropriate for us, especially for some of our princes and kings, who have betrayed us in the past by defecting to the enemy. The day when our impious act became known, many tears were shed at the holy church, and a great deal more by those we love. Even our infuriated companions threatened us with their swords, and were eager to punish us. Far distant people, who had heard of our Christian faith but were unaware of our secret intentions, mourned and unintentionally condemned us.

'There was a time when we were distressed in body and soul. Today, we are joyful and discreet, because we have with us our beneficent Lord. As we've long rejected doubtfulness, let fear also disappear from our hearts and minds, brothers. Neither the huge Sasanian army nor their war elephants will frighten us. The blow, wherever struck, must be sudden and heavy – always surprise the enemy. Until now, we have served mortal kings. It is time to serve the Immortal King. Let the good deeds of the Maccabees, who won their freedom of faith from the Seleucids, be an example to you all. However, I promise you and myself additional wounds, bruises, scars and death, rather than rewards. But be assured that through these wounds, Armenia will be free to worship Christ.'

Fists raised, the Armenian soldiers, who had listened intently, supported Vardan with loud shouts: 'Long live our great commander!'

The speech instilled inspiration, and stimulated Vardan's troops towards defending not only their religion, but also their culture, and entire way of life. Even women, helmeted, swords in belts, and shields in hands, were ready to fight and die for freedom of faith.

Chapter 20

In the early hours of the next morning, the two armies – one led by Vardan, the other by Mushkan – lined up on the opposite sides of the Tghmout tributary of the Arax River.

Priest Ghevont celebrated the Divine Liturgy on the plain, and distributed Holy Communion to Vardan and every soldier. He baptized those who had not yet been baptized in church, after which they all sung and prayed with fervour, reciting the 23rd Psalm in one voice.

> 'The Lord is my shepherd; I shall not want.
> He makes me lie down in green pastures.
> He leads me beside still waters.
> He restores my soul.
> He leads me in paths of righteousness
> for His name's sake.
>
> Even though I walk through the valley
> of the shadow of death,
> I will fear no evil,
> for you are with me;

your rod and your staff,
they comfort me.

You prepare a table before me
in the presence of my enemies;
you anoint my head with oil;
my cup overflows.
Surely goodness and mercy shall follow me
all the days of my life,
and I shall dwell in the house of the Lord
forever.'

The soldiers then took an oath to fight the enemies of the truth, saying: 'We're ready for persecution and affliction, and to die for the sake of the holy churches, which our forefathers entrusted to us. In the same way, we want to renew ourselves spiritually, for we recognize the Holy Gospel as our Father.'

The priest then delivered a stirring and eloquent sermon, enhancing the love for their faith and their country. 'Neither the Persian forces nor death could undermine our union with the Lord.' These were the last words of the religious leader.

The troops rejoiced and cried out, 'May God look down in mercy upon us and may He protect us from the hands of the evil enemy!'

Vardan's army (66,000 soldiers), a combination of veterans of the Sasanid wars with Rome and Iberian/Albanian joint forces, was positioned on the north bank of the river. Accompanied by some clergymen to conduct services for the first time, a section of Vardan's troops were foot soldiers equipped with bows, swords, and spears. The Armenian commander had organized his army into four divisions: the Khorkhoruni and Vanandian forces, under the command of their generals, led the left and right flanks; at the centre were the Artsruni forces; and Vardan himself took personal command of the combined infantry and cavalry corps.

Mushkan's Sasanid army (260,000 soldiers), outnumbering the Armenians almost four-to-one, and consisting of contingents from Caucasian/Central Asian territories and 40,000 warriors under Vasak Siuni, was deployed on the south bank of the river. The army's centre were the Immortal elite corps of 10,000 cavalry cataphracts – known as the javidan – who were heavily armoured and equipped with swords, javelins, and lances. The corps were reinforced at the rear by a squadron of armoured elephants, and each elephantry unity carried an iron-clad tower, within which was a contingent of bowmen. Mushkan himself rode the animal with a barbed tower, to command a full view of the entire battlefield and direct force movements.

The first attack was by the Armenian warriors, as Vardan drew his sword, shouting: 'Charge!'

His soldiers impetuously crossed the river, raising a cry: 'It is the will of God!' and creating a violent and heroic beginning of the fight.

Thus, both sides, seized with a mighty rage, roared as they rushed against each other south of the river, in fierce hand-to-hand combat.

Warriors of the Immortals taunted the Armenian soldiers with harsh chants: 'Mard o mard' (Man to man) as they flashed thousands of swords and raised countless spears. One could hear the clangour of the shields, and the snapping of the bow strings.

In this great confusion, while some soldiers became frenzied and deserted the battlefield, the brave ones dashed forward courageously.

The Armenian Khorkhoruni and Vanandian forces of the left and right-wing divisions, together with the non-partisan Artsruni forces in the centre, attacked the enemy's positions. 'Keep on fighting!' their generals encouraged them. But they failed to advance, and retreated after the Sasanids broke their ranks.

Vardan, having noticed their retreat, hurried with his cavalry corps to help gather the Armenian ranks. He retrieved the situation on the ground with some success. After that, the right flank of the Armenian forces faced a counterattack by the right wing of the Sasanids' cavalry. Vardan immediately intervened with his backup cavalry units. 'Full speed ahead!' he charged. He then battered the Persian warriors, thus rescuing his men from the counterattack.

The Persian corps, dislodged from their position, were put to flight without being defeated. Mushkan rallied his troops and committed his vast reserves, of which Vardan had none. The latter then attacked the "army of elephants", where he saw Vasak Siuni – the traitor – fighting against his own compatriots. He struggled to reach him, while Vasak sheltered behind one of the tower armoured elephants. 'Come out of there!' Vardan shouted at him.

Three of the bowmen in the tower snatched an arrow from their quivers, and shot them towards Vardan, but he quickly swung his horse around and the arrows missed him. He rode away, unharmed.

The Armenian commander, along with his top officers, climbed to the top of a small nearby hill to examine the entire battlefield. As they watched the Armenian and

Persian troop movements, they realized that the former were advancing on one front, causing the enemy considerable casualties, but were in retreat on the other, as the Sasanid general unleashed his elephants, breaking the Armenian lines once more.

Under the violent shower of arrows and spears, Vardan and his officers were hit, the latter falling heroically to the ground amid the dreadful carnage. The commander was seriously injured, and in his last agony he recalled the words he had addressed to his troops at the end of his speech. 'I promise you and myself wounds, bruises, and death. But be assured that through these wounds, Armenia will be free to worship Christ. I surrender my life to you, Lord.'

Vardan murmured in pain and died.

Since there was no longer any commander around whom the remainder of the Armenian troops could rally, they dispersed, but went on to capture strongholds and fortresses.

Chapter 21

At sunset, when the fighting ceased, the dead bodies of the slain, not fully identified, were thickly heaped together, with broken spears and shattered bows strewn all over the field. The bodies reflected the ravages of weapons, of human conflict, and the effects of exposure to the sun. Some soldiers, who were still alive, suffered from serious spear and chest wounds. Moreover, casualties included those who had been psychologically damaged by warfare, and those who had suffered from non-combat-related diseases. There were no national cemeteries, and no burial details.

In one day, 1027 Armenians had perished: 287 warriors, including Vardan, his eight officers, and 740 others of the royal house of Artsruni. During the battle, a number of Armenians lost their lives as they were trampled to death by the war elephants.

On the side of the Sasanians, around 3500 died, including nine distinguished officers, whose loss Mushkan mourned, and he paid tribute to them. Although the Persian general miraculously survived from heavy wounds, he was greatly upset at the huge losses his army had suffered in the battle.

As a punishment, traitors to his army and enemies of the Sasanid empire were crushed to death by the elephants.

Nobody exactly knew who had won and who had lost the war. Although the Armenians had some initial military success, they won the war in terms of casualties. While their total loss was over 1000 warriors, the Sasanian side sustained about three-and-a-half times more heavy losses.

During a period preceding the Battle of Avarayr, Vardan had waged a number of military campaigns against the Sasanids. The Armenians had a chance of victory now, if the results of those wars fought in 450 AD had been appreciated by Armenia's nobility, and if the latter would have taken the Persian army defeat as an opportunity to re-strengthen their forces for the upcoming battle. Unfortunately, a lack of unity and strategic planning among the nakharars had a baneful effect on the Armenian army for a positive outcome.

In conclusion, Armenia gained a moral victory, as it stood up to a mighty enemy that eventually failed to impose the heathen religion on the Armenians, whereas the Sasanians gained a military success in the technical and strategic sense, as the top Armenian generals, along with Vardan, died on the battlefield.

However, the battle of Avarayr was not decisive, as the Armenian population rose up again and held a massive rally against the Persians, who had harassed and pursued the remaining Armenian leaders. As a result, many noblemen sought refuge away from their fiefdoms.

At this point, the land was in turmoil, with internal lawlessness and anarchy. Yazdegerd opened an investigation into the causes of the havoc, but all in vain. A group of Magi Zoroastrian priests came to Yazdegerd's court, and petitioned the king to take drastic steps against the Armenian clergy.

One of them said angrily, 'They were the whole cause of the misfortune that befell the Sasanian army, which suffered three times more casualties than the Armenian army.'

Another Magian added, 'Their priests should have been long put to death.'

'Have they incited the people against me?' the king asked, stupefied.

'They surely did.'

By the order of the king, they were all arrested, along with priest Ghevont, churchmen, the patriarch, and other companion priests. Imprisoned, they were condemned to death, then executed in cold blood. These executions outraged the Armenians, who wanted to rebel against this slaughter. Aggrieved, they all gathered round their new commander, Vahan Mamikonian (Vardan's nephew), to listen to what he had to say. After holding a minute's silence to pay tribute to the dead, Vahan declared solemnly, 'I understand your grievances. At present, we have no choice but to organize our local resistance and take revenge for our martyrs.' He continued, with determination raising his voice, 'We will fight the enemy to the death.'

The Armenian rebels shouted unanimously, 'To the death!'

The commander then led the Armenians in a guerrilla war that would continue to rage in the Armenian highlands.

Meanwhile, Vasak Siuni, the fugitive and traitor, who had hidden among the war elephants, hurried to the Sasanid commander and showed him various stratagems, whereby he might take the enemy's fortified castles.

Following the complaints lodged by Armenian leaders of the uprising against the deceit and intrigues of Vasak, a royal court was held under the presidency of Mihr Narseh in early 452 AD. During the hearings, Vasak's old letters – all stamped with his own seal – to the Byzantine Emperor, to his general in Anatolia, and to the rulers of Georgia and Albania, asking assistance in the struggle against Persia, were introduced, together with more evidence, which made his double-dealing clear. Mushkan himself charged Vasak with disloyalty for, after the Avarayr battle, having betrayed many people with false oaths, luring them from their strongholds, of which he then took possession. Moreover, he found him guilty of peculation regarding state tributes.

A week later, the trial of Vasak resumed, as all dignitaries were summoned once more to the court. The accused appeared in full insignia as marzban, wearing a golden tiara and many honours of his rank. After a while, a chamberlain of the king's household appeared in the hall to question him. 'I come on behalf of the king to ask you from whom and for what worthy service did you receive all these distinguished honours?'

Vasak remained silent, for he knew he was now a victim of his own ambitions to be a king by ruse and treachery. The villain was entrusted to the jailor, who grabbed his medals in one palm and ripped them out of his golden robe, tearing a hole in the cloth. 'You don't deserve these,' he said harshly. Clothed with the garb of death, Vasak was taken to prison, where he fell seriously ill – his body shrivelled – and died. Because of his treachery towards Persia and his offences against Armenia, the king commanded that the place of Vasak's burial be kept a state secret.

Chapter 22

Yazdegerd appointed Adhur Hormizd as the new governor of Armenia. The king understood that, like his predecessors, not only had he failed in his initial policy to abolish the Armenian feudal system and centralize his empire, but he had further failed to assimilate the Armenians into the Mazdian religion. He was amazed by their firm and stubborn belief in the Christian faith.

The king issued a royal edict granting permission for all Christians, namely Armenians, to rebuild their churches and re-establish all things as before, so that they could practise their faith in freedom from then on. In the hope of regaining the good will of his subjects, he also curtailed various taxes. Although the king's edict was executed by Hormizd, in collaboration with Mushkan, the people's confidence was not immediately restored, because of former deceptions. Eventually, God secured a moral victory for all Armenians and Christians alike.

In 453 AD, towards the end of his rule, Yazdegerd moved his court to Nishapur – the second-largest city of Razavi Khorosan – to face the threat from the Huns, and left Mihr

Narseh in charge of the Sasanian Empire. The king spent many years waging wars against the Huns, to secure the northeastern portion of his empire against the enemy incursions. He also fortified the city of Damghan, and turned it into a strong border post. After his wars against the Huns, he shifted his focus to Armenia, Caucasian Albania, and the Roman Empire. Yazdegerd died in 457 AD without appointing a successor, instead entrusting the task to the elite. Civil war soon followed, and the empire, falling into a dynastic struggle, became divided.

Yazdegerd's son, Peroz, who disputed the rule of his elder brother, Hormizd III, took the throne after a two-year struggle. The new king, like his father, did not attempt to convert the Armenians and Albanians to Zoroastrianism.

Following the Armenian defeat at the battle of Avarayr, the scholar/chronicler Yeghishe, who had taken part in the war of religious independence, described in amazing detail the harsh and onerous period of the battle. Known as a strong adherent of the fifth century Armenian Church at its peak, he became the only national militant force in Armenian politics, taking an eclectic approach to righteous resistance.

However, Yeghishe renounced military life, and retired to the mountains, south of Lake Van, to become a hermit. In 464 AD, he made the acquaintance of a priest named David Mamikonian, who asked him to write about his experiences in the Battle of Avarayr – with its antecedents and aftermath – and the scholar willingly agreed.

In his work, which covered the period 428-464 AD, the author first acknowledged that the battle of Avarayr served as the nub of what it meant to be Armenian. He addressed an audience which was intellectually and culturally very varied. Most of them would be illiterate – the rest semi-literate – and completely unfamiliar with philosophical matters. Others still would be under the influence of paganism, or widespread popular beliefs.

In his account of rebellion against the Sasanians, he highlighted the critical role played by the lower classes. Carrying rationalism in religion, he concluded that misfortune came upon the Armenians as a result of ill education, and sins committed in the past. According to him, Armenia suffered greatly due to the bone of contention between its two neighbouring major powers –Byzantium and Persia. As a result, Armenian allegiances had not been consistent, neither in support of a coherent internal policy, nor with regard to external diplomacy. Under those circumstances, the Sasanid officials were astonished by how Armenia maintained its economic power even after the enormous increase of taxation.

Yeghishe established a framework of political analysis into which he referred to the character of Yazdegerd II. In his words, he said that one day the king was a "ferocious bull", on another day a man of "sweet disposition … who would humble himself from a haughty arrogance." He highly criticized the Zurvanite Zoroastrianism that the Persians tried to impose on his people. He included in his narration the myth of Zurvan, and a letter written by Mihr Narseh to the Armenians, emphasizing the importance of the myth.

The author then outlined an example that became the ideal prism through which Armenians endeavoured to survive and preserve both their identity and Armenia as a Christian nation. His text conveyed a polysemantic approach, as he described how a brave community, despite the odds, attempted to retain national unity and defend its language, culture, history, and religion. The author emphasized that unity was the mother of good works, whereas disunity caused evil deeds.

In fact, as the Armenians realized that they were in great danger of losing their identity, they all united against their common enemy for the first time – a clear reference to the pro-Roman and pro-Persian clans, with the exception of Vasak Siuni and his partisans. The treacherous attitude of Vasak and other renegade nakharars was condemned by the author as an act of treason, deserving fire and brimstone. Yeghishe aimed to immortalize the "heavenly courage" of the Armenians, and to give consolation to friends. He said: "Death, unanticipated, is mortality; death, anticipated, is immortality." He employed military knowledge of the tactics the Armenians and Persians used during the battle.

The book *History of Vardan and the Armenian War*, which he called a "recollection", came to be known as one of the typical works of the Armenian "best" literature. After Yeghishe's death, his remains were removed and taken to the Monastery of the Holy Mother of God, located at the shoreline of Lake Van.

In 474 AD, after several decades of ardent labour, Movses Khorenatsi completed his own work – a three-volume set called *History of Armenia*. At the end of his Third Book, he expressed his grief in a lament over the loss of his two masters – Mesrop and Isaac. He dedicated his work to Sahak Pakraduni, who was appointed marzban of Armenia by the Persians in 481 AD. When Movses heard that Sahak was later put to death because of his rebellion against them, he grieved over the loss of the gracious prince. The author entered the annals of history, and his three books earned him the epithet of "The Father of Armenian History". He was later referred to as the "Armenian Herodotus" by modern scholars and historians.

Ghazar Parpetsi was also a chronicler and historian, with close ties to the Mamikonian noble family. A friend of Vahan Mamikonian as well, he was best known for writing the history of Armenia from the fifth to early sixth century AD. Ghazar called his work, which was composed of three parts, covering the period 387- 485 AD, *Third History of Armenia*.

A fourth Armenian history chronicler of the middle fifth century was Pavstos Buzand (Faustus of Byzantium), whose work embraced an historical period from King Khosrov III Kotak until the partition of Armenia in 387 AD. Pavstos believed that divine intervention was not only related to strictly religious matters, but also involved in political and military affairs. He described two major dilemmas about the troubled political course of Armenians at that time. The first was the highly individualistic tendencies of the Armenian feudal lords, when the Armenian court endeavoured to centralize power for unity. The second was the difficult task of making a choice in relation to their powerful neighbours – the Persian/Roman/Byzantine Empires. This resulted in political disagreements, which caused dissention and even armed conflicts between the great feudal families.

Epilogue

In 481-482 AD, under the leadership of Vahan Mamikonian, the Armenians had continued a three-decade-long struggle against the Persians, in the form of guerrilla warfare from their strongholds in Armenia's upper highlands. Vahan had impelled the Armenian resistance to remain staunch adherents to Christianity. He recalled sadly how Shushanik, the daughter of Vardan, had patiently borne the tortures and cruelty inflicted upon her by her husband, Varsken – an Iranian prince converted to the Zoroastrian religion. In 475 AD, on Varsken's strict order, she was executed in Tsurtavi (Georgia), for having refused vehemently to abandon her Christian faith.

Vahan now managed to involve more forces in his army, reinforcing his ties with the Georgian rebels under King Vakhtank. He first took the ancient city of Dvin – the seat of the marzbanate. A year later, he defeated the Persian army in the battle of Nersehapat, which gained him a higher prestige. Although the joint Armenian-Georgian forces suffered setbacks in the battle near River Kura, their struggle continued.

The Armenian military strategy finally paid off with a policy of careful resistance against Persian control. After the death of King Peroz at the hands of the White Huns in 484 AD, his brother and successor, Balash, reassessed the long, indecisive conflict in Armenia, and sued for peace. Vahan sent envoys to the Persian camp, with proposals for religious freedom in Armenia. The main one was to worship in accordance with Christian doctrines, and for fire altars to be removed. Eventually, King Balash accepted Vahan's terms, and the Treaty of Nvarsak was signed in the same year between the Armenian rebel, Vahan, and representatives of the Sasanian King.

The treaty ensured religious freedom and greater political autonomy for Armenians. The conditions of the treaty were as follows:

1. All fire altars and temples in Armenia should be destroyed, and no new ones should be constructed.
2. All Christians in Armenia should have freedom of worship, and conversions to Zoroastrianism should be stopped.
3. Land should not be allotted to people who do not comply with the above-mentioned.
4. The Sasanian king should personally administer Armenia, not using deputies.

After the treaty was concluded, in 485 AD Vahan Mamikonian was recognized and appointed as marzban of Armenia by the Sasanians, and presented as an epic hero by all classes in the country. Subsequently, peace brought prosperity, and trade flourished, as the ancient town of Artashat became an important trading centre between the Byzantine and Persian Empires.

Ultimately, the battle of Avarayr – the Vardanian War

named after the sparapet Vardan – was then, and still is, seen as a cause and moral victory for the Armenians. It was something that had been rooted in the Armenian psyche for preserving and protecting the liberties of Armenia. The defence of the Christian faith by its people had been hailed as a landmark in the history of the struggle for religious freedom, and the fallen of Avarayr were held up as examples of heroism, patriotism, and Christian virtue to generations of young Armenians. Since then, Vardan Mamikonian, as supreme military leader – irreproachable patriot himself, and devout believer – had won the hearts of his people. Remaining steadfast in his Christian faith, he had surrendered his life to the Lord when, in his late fifties, he fell on the battlefield, and died.

The leader had put on all the armour the Lord gave to him, so that he could defend his faith, and fight against the evil forces and rulers of the dark Mazdian world. Vardan had let the truth be like a belt around his waist, his faith like a shield, and the Lord's saving power like a helmet. In return for his true struggle against Mazdaism, the Lord had preserved the identity of the Armenian people. Comparing the Armenians' struggle to that of the Jewish Maccabees, who successfully defeated the Seleucid tyrant Antiochus IV, the two followers of the Bible had fought for the right to worship in the face of religious oppression. In both cases, the prolonged struggle ended in a negotiated settlement assuring those rights, and produced martyred heroes.

The Mamikonian dynasty began to gradually decline in the sixth century AD, and came to an end during the eighth century, when the Sasanians were replaced by the Arab rulers of Persia. The Mamikonians rebelled against the Arabs, but were ultimately defeated in the battle. Almost all of the family's domains were lost, leaving only a portion of the southern Tarawn as a collateral branch.

Vardan was made a saint by the Armenian Apostolic Church. Although he became known as the most revered figure and important icon linked to Armenian identity, his generals, priests and companions are remembered with their leader on the feast day, for they were all killed; "martyred" was the term used thereafter by the Armenian Church. Shushanik was also regarded as a martyr, and canonized by the Georgian Orthodox Church and, among others, venerated as a saint, in the Armenian Apostolic Church.

In February of each year, Armenians celebrate the feast of Vardan and his companions – *Vardanank* – commemorating both their great rebellion and war against Persian tyranny in 451 AD. The feast is the most important national and religious holy day. Together with the battle of Avarayr, which has gone down in Armenian history as the greatest spiritual victory, the feast is celebrated by Armenians all over the world, with pride and respect, as a personification of the freedom of thought, faith, and conscience.

The Vardanants Day eternalizes the memory of 1036 soldiers of the Armenian army and their commander, who all perished at the Battle of Avarayr – a battle for the preservation of the Armenian Church, and Christian values. Preceding the feast of Vardanants is the feast of the Ghevontian saints, who gave their lives for their faith and their nation. Those brave, martyred churchmen, including their leader, Ghevont Yerets, who were also fighters on the front lines in the Vardan War, with a cross in one hand and a sword in the other, showed evidence of their character as ideal clergymen.

Notes on the Main Characters

Vardan Mamikonian, also spelled Vartan, was born in 387 AD, the year of the partition of Armenia.
Tiridates III is also known as Tiridates the Great, or Tiridates IV, to distinguish him from another Tiridates thought to have ruled several years earlier.
Gregory the Illuminator, a Parthian noble of Arsacid lineage, is the first official head of the Armenian Apostolic Church.
Mesrop Mashtots is a Medieval Armenian linguistic, theologian, and hymnologist.
Yazdegerd I, also spelled Yazdgerd and Yazdgird, is an old Iranian name.
Movses Khorenatsi, also written as Moses of Khoren and Moses of Chorene, is an Armenian historian from the period of late Antiquity.
Yazdegerd II is also given the title of Shahanshah, meaning King of Kings. Persian and Arabic sources claim that he conducted a religious devotion lifestyle. Whereas, in contrast, Armenian and Syriac sources describe him as a religious fanatic – the latter is stressed in modern historiography.

Ancient Religious Notes

Ancient religions had emerged from Ancient Near East and were mostly polytheistic. The peoples of Iran and of India had close historical links through the ages. They shared a common Indo-Aryan language and racial past. Containing common elements in their sacred books, mainly the Avesta and the Vedas, the religion of those peoples has been reconstructed. Both practised polytheism with the same gods – the Iranian Mithra and the Indian Mitra, along with the cult of fire.

The Mazdian and the Zoroastrian worships are regarded as two sides of the same coin. Mazdaism – more akin to the thought and faith of the Hindus – is a developmental stage that eventually led to Zoroastrianism. In other words, the religion that the prophet Zoroaster brought is a reformed form of ancient Mazdaism. The question of what the main building blocks of its original religion were, and how were they transformed into an amended structure, has been long debated by scholars.

On the other hand, Zurvanism – a hypothetical religious movement – is a branch of greater Zoroastrianism, in which the Zurvan divinity is a primordial creator deity, who engendered equal but opposite twins: Ahura Mazda and Angra Mainyu. Zurvan was perceived as the one and neutral god of infinite time and space, without any passion, for there was no distinction between good or evil for him.

There was a special role for the late Sasanian administration (438-450 AD) under Mihr Narseh, who supported the Zurvanite version of Zoroastrianism during the reign of Yazdegerd II.

As for Zoroastrianism and Paganism, the two are not the same. While the former is a monotheistic religion in the sense that its supreme deity is Ahura Mazda, the latter is a polytheistic religion – the worship of multiple idols/objects, which represent multiple deities.

Author's Viewpoint

The Armenians had been deprived of independent statehood for centuries. It was the misfortune of Armenia to often serve as a battleground for the antagonists. Eventually, the Armenians paid for the grave errors of political miscalculations in their lives. As a result, their country was subjected first to the rival claims of the Roman and Parthian Empires, and then partitioned, falling under the Byzantine and more dominant Persian influences.

The Armenians had been a defeated warrior and subject people, if I may put it, for they had not been with one voice when the existence of their domains was under threat in ancient times. As a perverse race, their greatest enemies were their incompatibility, incompetence, political immaturity, and discord. What they lacked most was astute leadership and political guile.

Such national weaknesses led to internal jealousies, strife, and betrayals during the most successful period of their national life. They were disrupted, and finally subjugated, but never assimilated as a nation. Their enemies, in order to control them, have made great use of those weaknesses, playing one party off against another.

It is true that the Armenians sometimes emerged victorious from the wars, due to their heroic strong will, proving that it is quite possible for the few to win against the many. But again, their efforts were ultimately bound to fail, and in the end they lost a big portion of their homeland.

A territory that had been the fatherland of the Armenians since 600 BC had shrunk at present to almost one tenth of its original size, due to invasions, incursions, and massacres. They were unlucky to be simply Christians and to think about nationalism.

Even today, Armenia – a landlocked country surrounded by enemies – faces many internal and external challenges, due to its leaders' political ineptitude and discord, although the country remains under Russia's so-called "security umbrella" and military wing.

Appendices

Appendix 1. The partition of Ancient Armenia in 387 AD

Appendix 2. The banner of Mamikonian dynasty

Appendix 3. The expansion of the House of Mamikonian

Appendix 4. The borders of Marzpanate Armenia

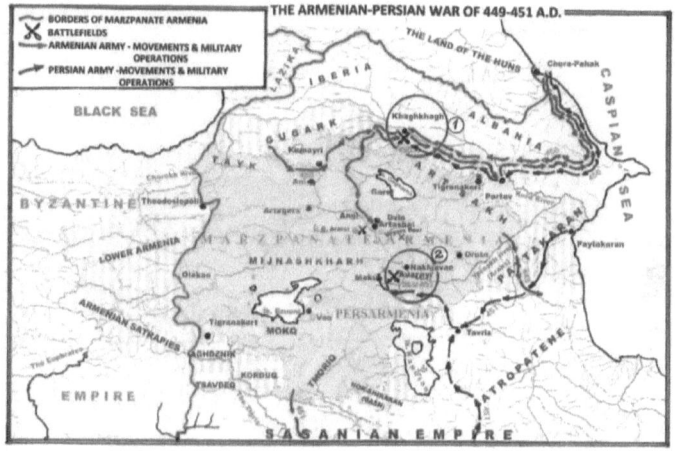

Appendix 5. Vardan Mamikonian

Appendix 6. Ghevont Yerets

Appendix 7. The battlefield at Avarayr in 451 AD

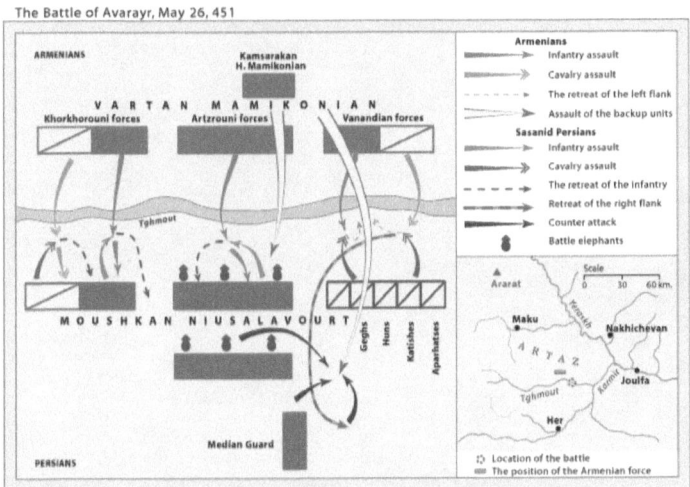

Appendix 8. Vahan Mamikonian

ՎԱՀԱՆ ՄԱՄԻԿՈՆԵԱՆ

Appendix 9. Tiridates III, King of Arsacid Armenia

Appendix 10. Gregory the Illuminator

Appendix 11. St Sarkis and his son

Appendix 12. Mesrop Mashtots

Appendix 13. Yazdegerd I, King of the Sasanian Empire

Appendix 14. Moses of Khoren (Movses Khorenatsi)

Appendix 15. Yazdegerd II, Sasanian King of Kings

www.ingramcontent.com/pod-product-compliance
Lightning Source LLC
Chambersburg PA
CBHW021149080526
44588CB00008B/268